The Write Path

Israeli and Palestinian Youth Finding Commonalities and Mutual Understanding Through Writing.

Steven Aiello and Bob Vogel
A Writers Matter Initiative

"If we are to teach real peace in this world, and if we are to carry on a real war against war, we shall begin with the children." **Mohandas Gandhi**

COPYRIGHTS

This book and its contents are protected under international copyright laws. All rights reserved. No part of this publication may be reproduced, distributed, or transmitted in any form or by any means, including photocopying, recording, or other electronic or mechanical methods, without the prior written permission of the publisher, except in the case of brief quotations embodied in critical reviews and certain other noncommercial uses permitted by copyright law.

ISBN: 978-1-964852-22-5

For permission requests, please contact the authors at:

vogel@lasalle.edu

debateforpeacemun@gmail.com

DEDICATION

This book is dedicated to the courageous Israeli and Palestinian teens who came together through writing amidst war, demonstrating that the pen is mightier than the sword. It is also dedicated to all the Israeli and Palestinian youth who continue to write their stories. We hope their empathy, compassion, and humanity will empower them to build a better future for tomorrow's students.

Steven's Dedication

To Dr. Dalia Fadila of blessed memory, who first believed in me as a teacher and who always said yes.

To my parents for teaching me to listen to different perspectives.

To my wife Daniela for your constant support and love amidst the chaos.

And, to my friends in Gaza, especially my dear friend G— you've taught me so much, shown me the true power of empathy. I'm praying for you and your families, and hoping that we can meet in person insha'Allah.

Bob's Dedication

To my colleague and friend, Dr. Sami Adwan, Ph.D., Professor of Education at Hebron University and Co-Director of the "Writers Matter Program" with me in Israel and Palestine from 2011 to 2018. Sami and I worked together to empower the voices of Israeli and Palestinian teens. My prayers are with Sami and his family, who live in Bethlehem and whose work with students has been hampered since October 7.

ACKNOWLEDGMENTS

Steven and Bob would like to acknowledge the following individuals and organizations who have made this initiative possible:

To the students and teachers who comprised the first cohort of the Writers Matter program, which began just weeks after October 7 amidst an ongoing war.

To the US Embassy in Israel for supporting Debate for Peace and for years of backing programs that bring people together.

To Risa Levy, Cultural Affairs Specialist at the US Embassy Jerusalem Public Diplomacy office.

To our major funders, whose encouragement, support, and funding made our vision a reality:

PTS Foundation: Tony and Pam Schneider

Berstein Family Foundation: Jeff and Dana Berstein

To Jonathan Kessler, founder of Heart of a Nation, who brought our stories to Washington, DC.

ABOUT THE AUTHORS

Bob Vogel, Ed.D.

Bob Vogel recently retired from full-time teaching after 43 years at La Salle University in the Department of Education and currently serves as Professor Emeritus of Education. He taught in public schools for three years before earning a doctorate in Educational Psychology and Organizational Development from Temple University.

In 2005, Bob became the Founding Director of Writers Matter (a 501(c)(3) nonprofit). The central mission of this program is to provide a unique and innovative opportunity for students in grades 2-8 to learn critical writing skills through personal journal writing, creating an opportunity to write about their lives at a time when expressing personal ideas and having their voices heard is so important. Since its inception, Writers Matter has served over 30,000 students. For more information about Writers Matter, please visit writersmatter.org.

Bob lives in the Art Museum section of Philadelphia with his wife. He enjoys opportunities for adventure travel, biking, hiking, and summers at the Jersey Shore. Spending time with his two sons, Jon and Dan, their wives, Kate and Katie, and his three granddaughters, Anya, Tally, and Mabel, is a priority.

Bob has co-authored numerous articles and several books, including:

Methods of Teaching: Applying Cognitive Science to Promote Student Learning (Feden & Vogel), McGraw-Hill, 2006

Voices of Teens: Writers Matter (Vogel & Galbraith), National Middle School Association, 2008

Empowering Young Writers: The Writers Matter Approach (Yost, Vogel, and Lewinski), Temple University Press, 2014

Writers Matter: Empowering Voices of Israeli and Palestinian Teens - Cultural Narrative Building through Writing (Vogel & Adwan), 2016

Society Unmasked: Voices of Teachers and Students in Unprecedented Time (Lewinski, McLaurin, and Vogel), Writers Matter, 2021

Wondering: Feelings, Emotions and Building Resilience (Vogel), Palmetto Publishing, 2023

Taco Tuesday: Stand Tall, Stand Strong (R. Vogel and M. Vogel), Amazon Publications, 2024

For more information, please visit bobvogel.org or writersmatter.org.

Steven Aiello

Steven Aiello is a Jewish Italian-American-Israeli. He grew up attending ultra-Orthodox Jewish schools in Brooklyn, NY, before studying for 18 months of post-high school yeshiva in Israel. He became an Israeli citizen in 2009, completed a master's in diplomacy, and served for two years in the Medical Corps of the IDF before returning to school to study Islam at Tel Aviv University.

In 2017, he founded Debate for Peace to bring together Arab and Jewish youth in Israel via Model United Nations, providing opportunities for talented and motivated youth to share their perspectives. The program has since grown to include students from the West Bank and abroad in over 100 cities and towns. Steven has run over 30 MUN conferences for approximately 5,000 students and led over two dozen Jewish-Arab youth delegations, including winning Best Small Delegation at YaleMUN 48 and Yale Model Government Europe 12.

Steven is an executive board member of the NGO CSD-NY, regional coordinator for Creating Friendships for Peace, dialogue facilitator for Asfar, an intercultural education NGO, and Middle East regional co-coordinator for the Bosch Alumni Network (BAN). He is passionate about sports, travel, debating, Model UN, reading, and comparative religion. He lives in South Tel Aviv with his wife, Daniela, and their dog, Waya.

He also shares writings from Gazan youth on his blog: blogs.timesofisrael.com/author/steven-aiello.

Contact:

Bob: vogel@lasalle.edu

Steven: debateforpeacemun@gmail.com

STUDENT AND TEACHER BIOS

Michelle

Michelle is a 19-year-old Persian girl who left Iran at the age of 12 and moved to Israel to live a better and safer life in freedom.

Abedalrhman Kais

Abedalrhman Kais is a 17-year-old Palestinian Muslim boy who lives in Karmiel in northern Israel. He enjoys listening to music, reading books, and writing articles on philosophy in his free time. He aspires to become a philosophy professor one day. He also loves hiking, playing with cats, and visiting museums and art galleries.

Tomer Donde

Tomer Donde is a Jewish Israeli who grew up and still lives in Netanya. Tomer likes to travel, play the violin, watch Star Trek, read, and ski. He studies Economics and Political Science in the Higher Education High School program.

Quds Ayoub

Quds Ayoub is a 17-year-old Palestinian Arab and Muslim girl originally from Nahef and Nazareth. She enjoys writing, public speaking, Model UN, traveling, baking, babysitting, nature, and animals, especially cats. Quds also likes meeting people, making friends, and getting to know new cultures.

Maia Rachel Klara Assaf

Maia Rachel Klara Assaf, a New York City native, embodies diversity as an American, Israeli, and Jewish teenager studying in Israel. With a passion for reading, writing, the beach, animals, and baking, Maia finds solace in creativity and expression. She is a history and literature enthusiast, constantly seeking knowledge and understanding. Maia prioritizes friendship over division and respect over politics, believing in the power of connection and empathy.

Yara Huleihel

Yara Huleihel is a 16-year-old Palestinian Arab Muslim girl who lives in Jerusalem, originally from the north. Yara enjoys playing soccer and volleyball. She also loves traveling, learning about new cultures, meeting new people, and spending time with her family and friends.

L. K.

L. K. is a 16-year-old Israeli-Jewish girl who loves to read and write. She also enjoys dancing, baking, and flowers. She is engaged in several community programs, such as Model UN, which includes meeting new people from around the world and debating current events, volunteering with kids, and managing community holiday events. Her studies are her top priority, as she is a top high school student and also a second-year BSC. Computer Science student at university. L. K. is curious and continuously explores her environment and abilities. She loves her family and friends more than anything.

Tamara

I'm Tamara. I was born in Moscow, and at the age of nine, my family and I moved to Sderot. On October 7, I was in Sderot, and these memories pursue me wherever I am. I believe that in the future, the younger generation will not experience what we are going through. We should all try to live in peace. It will not come right away, but we are the ones who can change the world for the better. In my poems, I wrote about life in Israel, and another poem with a hidden meaning.

Dana Khatsevich

I am Dana Khatsevich, a 17-year-old student from Israel. I was born and raised here, and I can gladly say that I am a proud Israeli Jew. I love my community and feel like it is my big family. I can see the passion in each person   and the fire in their eyes, trying to become the best versions of themselves. I want to be like them; I want to find my true passion and my own story. I had never written anything before this program, and I was skeptical about myself, but I am glad that I was willing to open my doors. I am very thankful for this amazing opportunity that opened my eyes. I discovered a new hobby I never thought I would have. I have space to improve, but there is always a starting point, and this is mine. I wanted to express my feelings and share what it is like to be a Jew and how hard but also beautiful it is to live here. What better way to do that than writing? I invite you to the beginning of my story, where I share my point of view on the world, and I hope you enjoy it.

With gratitude and love,
Dana

Amal Buqai Kayal

I live in the Holy Land, in a village called Judeida-l-Maker, close to Akko. I am a wife, mother, and teacher. I live in a place of peace that has no peace. I live in the land of prophets and messengers from God who taught creation what justice, peace, tolerance, and love are, but where people fight for decades to achieve them.

I strongly agree with the second Muslim caliph Umar bin al-Khattab's quote, "Sometimes the people with the worst past create the best future." No one on earth likes to suffer, live in war, or fight. We dream of living safely and peacefully and do our best to realize that what matters most is to work hard, not give up or lose hope, and be optimistic that everything will change for the better one day.

I believe that God created people with differences, and the test for each of us is to accept and respect others as they are. In this harsh, wild world, I try to be a helping hand to all who need help and support.

As you begin your journey through this book, you will encounter personal accounts of students experiencing war and finding ways to cope with this new reality.

Cover Artist

Special thanks to Ram Abo Ganeb, a talented young Druze student from the city of Maghar in northern Israel. In addition to drawing the cover, Ram contributed writing to the book as well, as part of the Maghar English Leadership program.

INTRODUCTION

On October 7th, the last day of the holiday of Sukkot, Israelis awoke to a living nightmare: thousands of militants had entered Israel from Gaza, overrunning towns and cities in southern Israel, marking the deadliest day for Jews since World War II. Over 1,100 were killed, and hundreds of men, women, and even young children were kidnapped and taken hostage. These events sparked the deadliest war in half a century for a region that has rarely known tranquility. As of this writing, over 40,000 people have been killed in Gaza, approximately 2% of the population of the Gaza Strip.

Beyond the numbers is the living human trauma. Nearly everyone on both sides of this conflict has deep personal ties—relatives or close friends who have been killed, kidnapped, or maimed, as well as those who have been through near-death experiences. Most Israelis and Gazans have experienced running to a bomb shelter or, even worse, not having any shelter or living too far from a safe place to seek refuge.

During the opening weeks of the war, Steven and his wife slept in a safe room as rockets lit up the sky. During this traumatic time, many peace activists felt despondent. It seemed like the rug had been pulled out from under them. The foundations of coexistence had been destroyed, and no one knew how to put them back together. At the same time, Steven felt an opposing pressure—the need to help and to bring people together. As the war forced students from school, with the support of the US Embassy, he began offering programming on Zoom. This became a safe space for Jewish and Arab students to continue meeting and talking. These programs started on October 10th, just three days after the war began, and lasted for over two months before in-person meetings could resume.

Dana Berstein, a mutual friend and supporter, serendipitously introduced Steven to Bob Vogel, Founding Director of Writers Matter in Philadelphia. Professor Vogel has years of experience in using writing to help students express their deepest emotions and deal with trauma, including in the Israeli-Palestinian context. They talked on Zoom and immediately decided to launch a writing program—the Writers Matter Israeli-Palestinian version. This group began with about 20 students and teachers, who met for weekly, hour-long Zoom meetings. Each week, Professor Vogel presented a new writing prompt. The following week, the writers would meet, share writing, and offer feedback.

It was critical that the sessions emphasized self-care and were not designed to be a place to espouse political views. We wanted to create a non-political and safe space for students to feel genuinely free to really open up about what they were experiencing. These sessions were designed to allow the students to talk about feelings, personal challenges, and coping strategies as they faced a new reality in their lives. One Jewish student wrote, "The sessions helped me find commonalities with other Arab students. We learned to better understand each other's feelings, hopes for the future, and even appreciate our differences. We were both afraid of the other's nationality but shared the same desire for better days." An Arab student wrote, "This program gave me strength and courage to express myself freely and honestly…everyone should join a program like this because they won't be scared or feel threatened by the other side."

The program lasted over two months and produced some amazing narratives and poetry that reflected how these students discovered personal resilience as they faced their new reality, which had been forced upon them. Eventually, as students gained confidence and pride in their writing, a public reading via Zoom was held for about 50 guests. Finally, with Professor Vogel's support, a group of student writers traveled to the US to read their work and discuss their experiences. These student writers met over 500 strangers in schools, universities, synagogues, churches, and young professionals' meetings.

Although the writing program was experimental—something new launched during an incredibly intense ongoing tragedy and trauma—it became one of the most meaningful projects in which any of the participants had been involved.

Teenagers seek meaningfulness in their lives, desire connections to their world, and a sense of personal responsibility for their learning and environment. The Writers Matter approach offers the students autonomy and opportunities to take responsibility for themselves. To help students believe that their ideas and actions can make a difference, they must be empowered. This means creating opportunities to express themselves in a supportive and trusting environment.

For students in the Middle East, anxiety is a product of their environment. The constant sounds of jet planes and helicopters overhead, gunfire, mortar shells, and bombings, compounded by checkpoints, house and car searches, bomb alerts, and the death of friends and relatives, create stress and inner conflict that children bear into adulthood. A supportive and trustworthy environment for these children to express themselves is paramount to their developmental growth and socialization. Without these opportunities, their notion of self-worth could be diminished, and their ability to develop self-confidence and a strong self-image could be compromised. Writers Matter serves as an antidote and a forum for children to safely express themselves.

As you begin your journey with this book, you will be provided with many personal accounts of students experiencing war and finding ways to cope with this new reality. Listen closely to their voices. You will learn about these students' personal resilience and how their openness to others who are different has enhanced their lives. By writing, they have found a pathway to raise their voices about life during war and express their dreams for a better tomorrow. The authors hope that you will learn important personal lessons from their writing.

WRITING ACTIVITY AND PROMPTS

This book captures the raw and piercing emotions that students (and teachers) have experienced since October 7th and the ensuing war. It offers a window into not one but numerous perspectives of ordinary people going through extraordinary trauma and reflects a range of personal experiences and reactions. While readers, teachers, and their students may not face similar circumstances, we believe that this writing experience can be useful to everyone. In addition to   sharing the prompts that were used, we encourage educators, writers, and others who are interested to reach out to us via email for recommendations on how to modify these prompts to fit your specific needs and situations.

The Writers Matter: Israeli-Palestinian sessions are structured to provide students with specific writing strategies and prompts to effectively communicate their messages and stories. Examples of writing from similar prompts and previous Writers Matter groups were provided to these students to help them formulate ideas for their own writing. These prompts leave ample space for individuality; students may choose to write their responses as narratives, stories, or poetry.

Throughout the sessions, students were encouraged to share their thoughts and write with each other in a safe place to share intense personal feelings and concerns. The result was not only powerful and reflective discussions but also fostered a community of learners. It also helped them realize they were not alone as they faced myriad frustrations, traumatic events, and feelings of loss of control when everything around them was in flames.

These sessions and writing opportunities gave the participants a pathway to share their feelings and for their voices to be heard.

Activities and Prompts

The following are some of the writing activities and prompts:

Activity One – This will help you focus on your thoughts, feelings, emotions, and reactions to the ongoing war and encourage you to express your personal perspectives and inner thoughts about living life every day.

Prompts

- What is one word that describes how you are feeling about the war?

- What has been most challenging for you since the war began (physically, emotionally, family, etc.)?

- How have you coped with your feelings and emotions about the war?

After all students respond, discuss the major themes that emerged. What was the tone of the responses? Were there similarities? Did you agree with many of your fellow participants? Which details have some students chosen to focus on? Was there a range of feelings and emotions expressed?

Activity Two – Using a visual organizer, brainstorm what you want to write about in your personal narrative. Collect as many ideas as possible in a random order that is important to you about your life and record them in any desired order. Once you have many ideas on paper that you want to write about, these will be available to you when you begin to write. This type of organizer allows you to think freely and place ideas in any order you prefer without feeling the constraints of structure. You can even create your own visual organizer if that helps you map out your ideas.

Suggested Activities

- **I Am From** "I Am From" provides an opportunity to explain who you are, where you come from, and what your life is like. You will be expected to write about yourself—how you introduce yourself to others, your personality, things you like and dislike, and how you value and see yourself with others. There are no right or wrong responses.

Step 1 – Read one or two examples of an "I Am From" to the students (examples are provided below, or you can write your own and share with the class. Writing your own will encourage trust and help to create a safe environment). Reading the work of others is also powerful and will encourage a comfort zone for students' work. Hearing students' voices that are similar and different from theirs will help get them started and, again, provide a safe environment.

Additional Writing Prompts

- **I wonder about** ... Students are encouraged to let their minds wander and wonder. Whether it's one question or a series of questions, big or small questions, about the past or the future, let the process of wondering guide the writing.

- **I wonder about Today, Tomorrow, and The Day After...** Here the wondering is framed by time, linking and contrasting the present, short-term, and long-term future.

- **We are From** This is a collaborative adaptation of "I Am From," in which two (or more) writers co-write a piece about where they come from. Other pieces can also be made collaborative.

- **Reflections** During the final session, participants are encouraged to reflect on how participation has impacted them.

It should be stressed that these are just guidelines; there is a great deal of poetic freedom for interpreting each prompt.

Contents

Chapter 1 - Personal Stories from the Onset of the War

A COLLECTION OF PIECES WRITTEN WITHIN THE FIRST FEW WEEKS OF THE WAR.

The Last Sleepless Night

The clock has already raced to the swift hour of five; I can feel the end of the day. I want it to be over. I stayed in my living room all day; it was the room closest to the shelter. I was lying supine on the couch; I hadn't moved in a long time. My legs wouldn't move. I was paralyzed. The television was on, but I didn't hear a word. I'm waiting for the alarm to go off.

It was raining. I thought to myself, maybe today will be one of those peaceful, beautiful days where all you can think about is running outside when the rain is over and smelling the petrichor of post-rain. My favorite smell. Somehow, I got up to get myself a drink. The glass was in my hand, I brought it up to my lips, and suddenly I heard a big shatter, a loud explosion. I felt a painful sting in my leg. I looked down, and the glass that was in my hand was all over the floor in small pieces.

But how? It was in my hand a second ago. Quickly, the shock was gone, and I realized what had happened. The alarm went off, and my body didn't react; fear took over. Barefoot and bleeding, I ran to the shelter. I locked myself in and fell to the ground. The only thing I thought about were the people who the rocket might fall on in their city, that this night might be the first sleep they won't wake up from. The first sleep they won't wake up to share their dreams with their loved ones.

I thought about the horror that the children, grandparents, babies, and toddlers have to witness and be in. I thought about the soldiers that risk their lives, the risk of not seeing their loved ones

1

again, the risk of not waking up and breathing, smiling, laughing, and loving again just so I can hide in my shelter and be safe so my life can continue, so I will smile, live, laugh, and love.

Twenty minutes of dreading hearing an explosion, twenty minutes of overthinking, twenty minutes of panic, and twenty minutes of fear had gone. It was time to leave the shelter. I decided to go out after a few minutes. I smelled the petrichor of post-rain, but this time, it was the worst smell I have ever smelled in my life. It was the smell of panic. It was also the smell of realization, the realization that this would again be a sleepless night and that it won't last anytime soon.

A FRAME OF ANXIETY

Feelings are screaming, repressed, trapped, overflowing, leaking. All that is repressed is about to explode, and it is all that was and all that happened. Thoughts running through my mind, and sweat pouring from my body, to drown me from the sharpness and intensity of insomnia.

I do not know how to act, for all that is in my mind is a sea of paper followed by an endless stream of scattered, hopeful words, without opportunities.

Some of them cry from the intensity and the obsession of talking, and others cry from the silence.

I honestly don't know why they are gathered here, inside a frame of nothing and everything.

There, here, and he?
He surrounds them, protects them from death or the death of life in them, the death of their soul so that she doesn't end up soulless, but while doing that he kills them more and more.

He suffocates them and revives them, kills and saves, he is the killer and the savior, the lover and the hater, he plays the role of the still sea at the end of which is a deadly waterfall.

Sweat, blood, and heat come together to tell a story about staying up for hours, about the eternal thought formed by the visceral, bloody, and intellectual longing for sleep like forbidden fruit.

I come closer and he turns away from me, all the convergence between my turmoil in my life crowded into a square in my mind and is about to explode.

He quickly turns into a stone that hinders me, the one who carries him, in my daily life, and causes me wounds. I get up to scream, to speak, to grow, but I soon see that he is much stronger than me, that he is louder than me, and that he does not hear me or even give me attention.

He closed me with walls as thick as the thoughts that are in them, the experiences they have gone through.

Even more than my bed which I have not seen recently. Even more than my valor for my refusal to give in to what is happening.

I do not know what is happening behind those walls, nor do I know what exists outside of them, but I know that behind those walls there is a desired tranquility.

I also know that everything that is desired is forbidden. My reality has become those walls, and everything that is within me is what is within them.

I have never achieved anything beyond it, nor have I touched the tranquility that might keep me away from it exploding, that might prevent me and keep me away from the hurricane of walls.

The biggest presence around me is the presence of excess, void, and emptiness, mysterious feelings for which I have not found a name, but they are all I find.

Trapped in my mind, in its most complete and most beautiful form, I will not originate it so as not to arouse doubts and doubts in the minds of those passing by.

Those who do not live in my mind, those who are not me.

How Am I?

When someone asks how I am, I pause, torn between two choices. Should I share the truth of my emotions of stress and fear that consumes my reality, or should I simply nod and say I'm fine, carrying on with my day? Although my inner self wants to break free and express the reality of my feelings, I often find myself saying, "I'm okay."

Do I truly want to burden them with the weight of my experiences? Do I genuinely want to articulate the pain, suffering, nightmares, and guilt that I experience each moment of every day?

When I finally return home after a long day, my head sinking into the comfort of my pillow, tears escape. I cry, confronted by the undeniable fact that no matter how much I suppress my emotions during the day, they are real, and they are a part of me. I cry because I'm scared and overwhelmed, helpless in the face of a situation where I can't even help my own people in Gaza, the very ones I cry and worry about daily. My sadness transforms into a deep sense of pity, and I feel powerless. While I shed tears over my thoughts, others are shedding tears because they've lost loved ones, endured injuries, or faced starvation.

It's difficult to concentrate on basic subjects in school. I sit there, struggling to hold back tears, gazing at my phone, waiting for the news that I know will haunt me for a lifetime. When I receive that news, something changes within me. I feel resentment toward friends I once considered my closest allies, teachers whom I looked up to. I catch myself and, in doing so, realize the gravity and difficulty of the situation. I need to stop. I have to put my phone away and distract myself, doing whatever it takes to divert my mind from the grim reality. However, despite my efforts, I'm haunted by guilt. As I lay on my comfortable bed at home, I feel guilt for those with no place to sleep, no roof over their heads. When I want to eat, I'm reminded of starving children desperately longing for something to fill their empty stomachs in Gaza.

So, the honest answer to the question of whether I'm okay is no. I'm not okay, and I fear things may get even worse. I can't even use my voice to educate people about it because the consequences would be severe and put me in danger. I'm petrified to leave my house and meet my friends, fearing that someone filled with hatred could end my life and the lives of other innocent people.

Dear Diary,

I haven't written on these pages since the seventh of October. Something happened that day—a horrible, indescribable, unimaginable thing. So horrendous that I don't think my mind has allowed itself to accept it. The reason I hesitated to divulge this information is that the minute I document it, there is no denying it. There is no wondering if this is a figment of my imagination. However, the time has come to yield to this reality.

On October seventh, at six-thirty in the morning, I took my pillow and covered my ears to block out an irritating noise. Only a moment later, my mother entered my room, her voice unflappable, and uttered the words: "To the bunker. Now." And I listened. I rose to my feet and let them lead me to a place my body could find without the aid of my brain.

After the advised waiting time, I walked back to my bed leisurely. Just fifteen minutes after the siren was heard, I drifted off, my eyes closed, with no worry in mind, for this has become customary for me. When I woke up, my life had gone back to normal. School, gym, friends. It was just another casualty we faced, living in a world that justifies antisemitism.

I wish that was the end. With most incidents, this was the case. Life went back to normal. But this time it didn't. It was the look on my mother's face when I woke from my slumber. The look of utter despair and trepidation in my mother's hazel eyes led me to the revelation that this was just the beginning.

I opened my phone, and my heart dropped; time stopped as I stood shocked. Roughly 2,900 Hamas militants infiltrated Israel from Gaza using pickup trucks, motorcycles, bulldozers, speedboats, and paragliders, slaughtering civilians and demolishing southern cities and kibbutzim. They were in Israel. In a country I once longed to leave. A country I saw as a temporary place of dwelling until I could return to NY.

7

But as though I were a mother cub seeing her child in danger, the urge to protect was overwhelming. They were here. In my country. In my home. My sanctuary. Over the next few weeks, Israel sank deeper into the pits of hell. Over 8,000 rockets were fired into Israel, over 4,800 civilians were injured, over 1,400 innocent individuals were murdered, and over 240 were kidnapped. An incalculable number of Jewish people live in fear of being attacked, raped, or killed just for their religion. At least 8,000 Palestinians are dead, and 0 Palestinians are "free."

And the truth is, I am angry. I am angry and terrified that I live amongst humans who justify the decapitation of infants as a means of retaliation. I am angry and terrified that around the world, people protest pro-Palestine, chanting, "From the river to the sea, Palestine will be free." but they see a hijabi and flee. I am angry that the Jews and the Palestinians are just pawns in the battle of the great powers. I am angry that we can't live in peace because the world wants us to fight. They want a good and a bad, a right and a wrong as they sit safely watching on their TVs.

I am angry that we claim to be Jews and Muslims, yet we do not abide by what the Quran and Torah say. "We have not created the heavens and the earth and everything in between except for a purpose. And the Hour is certain to come, so forgive graciously." (Quran 15:85). The Torah explicitly forbids us to take revenge or to bear grudges (Leviticus 19:18). It also commands us, "Do not hate your brother in your heart" (ibid. 19:17). Hamas fights in the name of Allah while the Quran 59:23 discloses that peace is one of the names of God himself. I am angry that humans use religion, a peaceful way of expressing beliefs, against one another.

I am angry that they said "never again," and not even a century later, we witness their lie. I am angry that humans are filled with malice, ignorance, and hypocrisy. Every day, I ask myself, how does one recover? How does one learn to accept the monstrosity that occurred and move on with their life? I still don't know the answer. I still don't know the answers to so many questions I asked because no one knows. No one knows when the hostages will be released. No one knows if this is just the beginning. No one knows what this means for the Jewish people.

But we do know one thing. We stand strong and united. We fight for our country, and we die for her. We provide and contribute tremendously. The love for our country knows no limit. It is not conditioned, nor will it ever be. We share a common goal for the Jewish people to have a place to call home.

So, I profoundly thank my country for keeping my spirit strong. I thank my classmates for letting their fear be shown, making the world less lonely as we all die a little inside. I thank my father for his uplifting jokes, from which I remember how much I love to smile. I thank my mother for nurturing me and giving me peace of mind while she holds a burden much larger than mine. I thank the soldiers who put their lives heroically on the line so that we can live to tell our stories to the world.

And then I stop being thankful. Because the truth is, the devil on our shoulders speaks louder than the angel. He tells us to be indignant and loathe one another. To find someone to blame. It's a convenient way. We should not carry the pain of others, be selfish, and turn our backs. Yet the devil is not victorious with us. We believe in our future, and we pray.

I pray every day. Every single day, I pray that Hannah Katzer will see her grandchildren again. I pray that Dafna Elikim gets to graduate high school. I pray that Kfir Bibas gets to celebrate his first birthday. I pray Avia's family knows how brightly their daughter's smile shone. I pray for my people's safety and that they understand that those who are no longer with us will never be forgotten. Their legacies will live on through memories and stories.

I don't know who exactly I am praying to, but I pray nonetheless. I never fully comprehended what Judaism was. Was it the Bible or maybe the holidays? Maybe it was something much deeper. My father told me he would discuss faith once I

9

understand what my religion is to me and once, I find God within me.

As much as it pains me to say it, the war made me realize my truth. Judaism, to me, isn't God. It isn't about whether I wear a skirt to be modest or go to the synagogue on Friday. To me, Judaism is my culture - it's my people. It's the land where I miraculously feel safe, even while in a war.

I say this to myself, to whoever might find my diary in the future: Fear is inevitable in times of corruption and sin. However, one thing I cannot stress enough is that we are not alone. We have a nation behind us. 20 million Jews who refuse to abandon hope. Life is full of doubts, uncertainties, and fear. But one unquestionable thing is that we, the Jewish nation, are infinite, extraordinary, and exceptional.

October 7 Memories

October 7, 6:30 AM: We awake to an inhuman shrieking. Not the sounds of the missile detection system—we'd slept through those. Not the Iron Dome interceptors—they were still to come. No, we awoke to the frantic screaming of Usdi, our 13-year-old Shepherd. Usdi hadn't climbed stairs in months because of her age and bad hips, but by the time I was conscious enough to poke my head out of the bedroom window, she'd dragged herself halfway up to the second floor bedroom in sheer panic and motherly instincts. I scooped her up, yelled for Daniela, and we headed down to the bomb shelter just in time (our other dog Waya yawning in indifference).

7:30 AM: I go to the Syrian synagogue near the house. We can hear rockets bursting in the sky, but no one is fazed. The synagogue is mostly elderly men and I can't be sure that they can even hear what's happening outside. Today is a holiday, the eighth and final day of Sukkot, known colloquially as "Simhat Torah" - a happy, joyous day. We pray, read from the Torah and dance with it, everyone gets several bags of candy (one month later I will have my first root canal, but for now I indulge), and go our respective ways. We walk the dogs and then it's time to head out.

12:00 PM: We arrive at our friends' Yemenite synagogue. Every year their synagogue has a holiday party that lasts hours. We've come to experience that, everyone eating, singing in Yemeni-accented Hebrew, carrying the Torah, or their own younger children, around in a circle, the kids waving flags and of course holding goodie bags. But rumors abound. People look worried, stressed. And some are not there - they've been called up for an emergency response to something unfolding in the south of the country, that much we know, or think we know. A week ago we marked 50 years since the country was caught off-guard in the Yom Kippur war. Has history repeated itself?

7:00 PM: The holiday is over and I open my phone to a flood of messages, friends from all over the world asking if I'm ok. My chat group with Gazans is buzzing, people expressing horror, fear, and mostly mutual concern. I'm trying to respond with one hand and eye while devouring the news with the other, each headline worse than the prior. We were supposed to go to a post-holiday party ("Haqafot sheniyot) at the Libyan synagogue in Jaffa, but when I ask if the party's still on, someone reacts angrily. I realize that my brain is still processing what's happening. There's a new reality and I need to adjust.

There are more bouts of rockets--we're lucky to have a bomb shelter in our new apartment. In my old place I never even bothered to go to the public shelter since it was too far and none of my neighbors could make it, so I just stayed home and prayed we'd be ok. But the next few weeks will be on and off rocket barrages, and we will sleep in the safe room for the first two weeks, when the salvos are daily. That first night we go to sleep still not fully aware of the extent of the catastrophe, still not fully comprehending what we do know, but filled with emotions. Isaiah 35:10 prophecies about a time when "agony" is turned to "joy." Today the opposite prophecy has been realized: joy has turned to agony. I go to sleep praying for tomorrow to be better. It won't.

Chapter 2 - I AM FROM

A POETIC LOOK AT WHO WE ARE AND WHERE WE COME FROM

I am from the hum of the Tel Aviv streets,
Where sunlight and laughter mix to vibrant beats.

I am from Shabbat candles' gentle glow,
In the warmth of traditions that elders bestow.

I am from the ancient stones of Jerusalem walls,
Echoes of history in every footfall.

I am from the melody of Mizrahi songs,
In the heart of nations where resilience belongs.

I am from the streets of Happy Sderot, where
kids walk alone without fear.

I am from the land where conflicts persist,
Yet, hope persists in the midst of the twist.

I am from the courage to rebuild and renew,
For after the storm, a brighter sky we pursue.

I am from a story still being told:
In the aftermath, our spirit unfolds.

***

I am from a limited wide, dark round space,

Captured by a long rope, in a complicated maze,

Trying to get to the exit, as fast as in a quick race,

Till I got to it and realized my mum's face.

I am from a family of warm love that gave me so much care,

That almost can't be found nowadays in this world of unfair,

Taught me to appreciate others, calling them ma'am and sir,

Taught me respect, and how to plant trees of hope everywhere.

I am from a society that follows the traditions of the old man,

Greeting others is a must, to make all people friends is the plan,

Taught me that friends are diamonds of Laura, Diana, and Hanan,

They are the tasty spices of life, and together we are the loyal fan.

I am from a place that plants good manners in the minds of small kids,

Teaching them that understanding and containing others kills the mess,

To achieve goals and realize dreams needs hard work to achieve success,

A place where educating people to be good members and decrease evil to less.

I am from a group of those who live in the space of
lovely homes and school,

Getting as much knowledge to educate members to
cancel the name of "fool" –

Who believe in the "love of power, not the power of
love" and get   it as useful tool.

Not tolerance is the weapon to break the limits to
get the light and feel so cool.

I am from then and now, from here and there,

From a place where its past is present everywhere,

Telling a lovely bedtime story to expel the
nightmare,

To relax worries with a smile and say "Thank you
sir."

I AM FROM

I am from a lazy, slothful morning.

Being lost in my mayhem of thoughts.

I am from a soothing, heavenly, melancholic melody from a song by Fairuz about a long-gone lover.

The melodies evaporate in the morning air as if they never existed.

I am from a circle of discontent.

A thought made of blood falls down, the ocean swallows it, it evaporates quickly and condensates, forming a new cloud.

And so on, the circle of bloody acid rain repeats itself unceasingly.

I am from a plate of Mulukhiyah being eaten on a random Sunday in January while it's pouring outside.

An ecstatic plate.

A segment of balance in the midst of disarray.

I am from Mahler 9

I am from a long walk in the autumn.

A cheerful song from the 80s that inspires me, a bewildered mind, a heavy type of guilt.

I am from meaninglessness.

A surreal painting that is unfathomably enthralling, a musical catharsis, a peculiar gemstone.

An oddly shaped flower.

I am from the unspoken words.

I am from the lost meaning.

I am from the unseen, unheard, and unloved.

I am from not belonging.

Feeling the weight of my shallow existence and never finding "home".

A lost one that perhaps, later on, I will try as hard as possible to compensate for losing it but I will never manage to.

I am from a shattered hope.

Billions of fragments, but reassembled, piece by piece because hope has to exist.

*****

I AM FROM

I am from the unknown, a lonely place.

I am from where emotions are concealed, hidden behind blank facial expressions.

I am from a world where the truth itself wears a deceptive mask.

I am from the right side of town but only when the other side is falling apart.

I am from a place that is constantly under war.

I am from a place that can't agree.

I am from a place where everything is always misjudged.

I am from a place where the cruelest of things happen.

I am from long workdays and endless sleepless study nights leaving me perpetually drained.

I am from exhaustion.

I am from harmful and dangerous false hope.

I am from a place where love is only in books, an illusion, where love is unwelcome.

I am from a place where love is a lie.

I am from a world where you need to change the word trust with betrayal.

I am from a place where trust is not real, everyone leaves, everyone lies, everyone cheats.

I am from a world where you can't talk, you can only guess, communication is a guessing game as words lose their power and silence prevails.

I am from where happiness is only something you can dream about, but the dream would be a lie because I am from a place where happiness is not a priority, happiness is not something we know. True happiness remains elusive.

I am from a place where stepping outside carries the weight of fear as judgment, whispers, and pointing fingers await.

I am from a place where the phrase "That's life" serves as a relentless push to endure rather than a comforting adage.

I am from painful and haunting unwanted memories.

I am from a place where you find yourself thinking the same thing every day "Was any of it even true?"

I am from where the length of a coat becomes a measure of self-preservation, guarding against the perils of the outside world.

I am from plastic smiles and fake crowds.

I am from where "Goodbye" is an excuse.

I am from a place where I am the constant source of comfort for others, but the sacrifice I make is seldom reciprocated.

I am from a place where your heart screams but your mouth fails to speak.

I am from a place where you stand up to fight or else it will be the last time you will stand.

I am from tricks and schemes.

I am from a place where deception and intrigue are the norm, and inked butterflies, semicolons, and medusas are the emblems of shared horrors.

I am from where people are characterized by responsibilities that weigh heavy on their shoulders.

I am from secrets, secrets that I don't want to find the key to unlock them.

*****

I am from ash.

I am from my blood, my skin.

19

I am from ash, clay, and just a little soul.
A little soul who makes mistakes,
A little soul who gets lost,
A little soul who does not know.

I am from mess and chaos.

I am from loving swimming, and remembering
drowning but...

I am from loving winter.

I am from loving nature, from looking outside my
window and admiring the beauty.

I am from the euphoria of swinging a little way too
high in the swing and feeling the whole world stop.

I am from hearing the sound of prayer next to my
house.

I am from my first cats, "Sukar" and "Loz".

I am from loving animals, or maybe animals taught
me how to love.

I am from olive oil.

I am from sitting under the olive tree for long
hours.

I am from sitting in front of my mirror for even
longer,
Looking, searching, checking in a broken mirror
too broken to see who I am.

I am from the politics of saying where I am from,
who I am, what I am, and what I want to be,
nowhere in the world does being who I am cause
dialogue, except where I am from.

I am from the confusion when anyone asks me what
I like, they want to know who I am "Just say what
you like."

I am from a world of individual people, within
groups, who maybe rely on these groups to get to
know themselves, who do not know themselves.

I mean you're only as deep as you have met yourself.

I am from all of my mistakes in the past and all of my decisions.
Maybe even I don't know what I like and want in life.
But I know I am from home.

I am from Jerusalem, my father's village up north, and my mom's city.

I am from reading, writing, and listening.
But when everything stops and no labels are around, I am Quds.
I am me, that's the only thing I will never lose, and that's what stays with me always.

*****

I AM FROM

If you ask me where I am from,
I'll remain silent and won't answer at all.
I would be staring right into the void,
Afraid to say something and regret it afterward.

If you ask me where I am from,
I'll imagine all the hurting souls,
Screaming and praying, trying to go back to their
homes,
Covered in blood and wounds,
Afraid to move to not get shot.

If you ask me where I am from,
I'll be frozen and won't move at all.
I would try to avoid my thoughts,
Because I know deep down,
That they are just lost hope.

If you ask me where I am from,
I want to shout out the name of my home.
I want to say,
I am from a beautiful place,
With a loving community and a welcoming hand.

I am from a beautiful place,
With shining smiles and unforgettable faces,
The place that I should never be afraid to
represent.

But what can I say? I'm afraid of everyone finding out that I am from Israel.

I COME FROM

I come from a place where everyone speaks their mind.

I come from a place where Jews can walk freely and safely.

I come from a place where everyone is from a different background.

I come from a place where we root for the underdogs.

I come from a place where the school teaches hate.

I come from a place where my parents tried to show a better way.

I come from a place where no one but us had dogs.

I come from a place where it's always too hot or too cold.

I come from a place that was always run down, but where we always had what we needed and got what we asked for.

I come from a place with good food.

I come from a place with bad music.

I come from a place where Jews are the majority minority.

I come from a place with many friends.

I AM FROM

I am from two different places, two distant realms.

Though not far away to travel, they don't let you keep calm.

Two different people, quite old and respectable.

Yet one line of hate and now formidable.
Two friends now gone, just despicable.

How can you sleep now? Who will be accountable?

Yet when I try to close my eyes, I think maybe that was not home.

When I sleep, I see a third place quite far, you need to roam.

So far away actually it's really a new kingdom.

Also, old and mighty, that is what I call home.

How can I pick, it's impossible.

Very close in mind, two facing the same goal.

Keep the boat afloat, indeed respectable.

Where am I from?

I cannot choose, yet all I have to do is to listen to my soul.

So simple yet so hard, too difficult a task, just undecidable.

Where am I at, that's what they really ask.

Two places shattered just like glass.

But when the time came, it was the 'H hour'.

They all committed to recover.

So, in the end, they ask you the wrong question at all.

It's not where am I from? It's where can you stand tall?

I AM FROM IRAN

I am from one of the oldest countries in the world - the country which invented human rights.

A country with a great history known for its beauty, culture, food, amazing people, and many other great things.

However, Iran didn't stay like that forever.
Where I am from is the country that steps on every human rights policy and destroys anyone who speaks against its government.

Iran isn't ruled by the greatest kings anymore, only by a bloodthirsty regime that kills its own people or sells weapons to other countries to kill other innocent people.

Where I am from, people aren't happy; they are suffering from inflation.

They are suffering from seeing that every day, someone gets executed for speaking against the regime.
I miss where I am from.

I miss my family, who I can't visit because I know if I go back, I can get arrested.

I miss where I am from because every weekend, every event, or every holiday, I used to gather with my big family, aunts, uncles, grandma, cousins, and family friends.

There were stories, there was music, and the feeling that you belonged.

Where I am now isn't where I come from, but Israel is a promised land, the land where you feel like you belong. Israel isn't my real country, but it's treating me better than my own country.

Where I am from, you don't miss anyone because they're already there.
But where I am now, I miss everything and everyone.

I AM FROM

*I am from a loving family that has always been my
biggest support system and taught me how to be a
human who respects all before anything else.*

*I am from a grandma who, when anything goes
wrong, will be the first I call, or when I need help
with my studies, she stays up until midnight to
make sure I understand everything.*

*I am from a mom who always tells me to care about
my education more than my looks because my
brain is what's gonna help me help my people in
the future.*

*I am from the olive tree that symbolizes strength,
life, wisdom, peace, and friendship.
It continues to grow even at the hardest of times
and has always given me some kind of hope.*

*I am from a school that taught me how to feel safe
and have a heated dialogue with the other side
despite our differences, and I am from a school that
always gave me an opportunity to share my voice
with outsiders and join programs like these.*

*I am from seeds of peace that somehow put my
mind at ease.
I am praying for peace and patience to all, yet I
still find myself between two walls.
Although I wish that I could continue with the
happy thoughts, I have to face reality and
remember that I am also from fake friends who are
willing to only take and put you at stake, and from
mothers whose hearts will always ache.*

*I am from where innocent lives are taken every
day, from my people and my land occupying my
mind and my heart, and from not feeling happy
until my community and I are no longer apart.*

27

I am from where not talking about your people and their suffering is considered being a traitor, and where talking about them can force you out of school or your job.
I am from where hearts are broken day and night and children may not be able to see another day of light.

Finally, I am from a very bad place where you reach a point where you live in guilt because "who are you to survive?"

Chapter 3 - I Wonder

THE LIBERATING EXPERIENCE OF WONDERING
I WONDER

I wonder why people miss their belongings and choose to get emigration.

Why do they kill moments, lose memories, and cause one's immigration?

I wonder if birds are cleverer than people to look for warmth by migration.

Enjoying the cool sun, and lovely moments without losing the direction.

I wonder why learners get sad when they fail and have no preparation.

I wonder why people suspect everything from God but they are still creation.

Life and death are two stages that every one of creation must try and pass.

Each is once. I wonder why people do not spend life as easily and so nice.

Worries are found, why they don't ignore them by jumping on the grass.

I wonder...
Why do people color their hearts black when they can be clean as glass?

I wonder why people go so deep in water while they fear one wave.

I wonder why roses are not found in far places of wild, wide-open cave.

I wonder about those who tease others and call for help to stay safe.
I wonder about so many things…
That may be answered after I will be taken to my grave.

I Wonder

I used to wonder if the phrase "Any relationship without trust is like a car without fuel, it can't move ahead" that I heard through my house walls constantly was true.

I used to wonder what trust is, who I should trust, and if trust is a feeling, a sentiment, or simply an excuse.
With time, I came to understand that trust is a double-edged sword. A weapon. Trust makes you blind, impulsive, and delusional, or maybe it's merely a false sense of security.

I wonder if anybody else thinks that trust is the way to get hurt and disappointed.

I wonder what made me incapable of trusting others again. Wait, I do know. It's the trepidation you get while wondering what will happen. It's the false hope you give yourself, thinking it will be different this time.
The fear of wondering what will happen when giving someone your heart glass and then dropping it and shattering it. Again.

Within each fragment of the broken heart lies memories, fragments of a bygone era that once completed the whole. I wonder if I put the pieces together, they will fit smoothly like a puzzle and complete my heart. But maybe some pieces changed their shape on the way down, and they fit into another puzzle.

I wonder if the fear will ever dissipate. But why would it? Why would I relinquish all my defenses to be manipulated again? Why would I give someone the power of my trust to their advantage again? Why would I offer myself entirely only to be discarded into the pit they have created? Again... I wonder who decided that trust is a mandatory thing. Who says that we need to trust others? What is their reason? Why can't we live without it?

I wonder what happens when other people look deep within their core. Do they feel the heat of longing that has been denied for so long? Or did they raise their hands and let that longing in?
Do they feel the voids that echo, empty and incomplete? The ash of passion smoldering inside.

I wonder if I am lying to myself and if I am the one who raised her hands. I wonder if I am the one that gave up...
When I look deep into my core, I see the girl that was left broken. I see her holding a jar with dozens of different broken glass pieces.

I wonder, if the little girls and boys that pinky promised their friends that they wouldn't tell their secret and did it anyway, how do they feel? Do they stop and think about how their friend feels? They are just little kids who don't think it through, so we all don't think much of it, but what about adults? I wonder why I wonder. Do they merit my pondering over their actions, investing my time to understand without harboring anger?

I wonder if I will ever wake up, look at the world, and think that maybe today is a day that it's worth trusting. I take one of my wonders back. I found the answer. I don't wonder anymore why I can't trust others - it's just I won't. Some may lament the absence of a completed puzzle with each new piece, but I view it as a reduction in effort.

PRAECEPTA

In Praecepta, a town so humble, embraced by the sea,

there emerged a lad named Wonder, a soul untamed and free.

His days were devoted to questioning all he'd see,

the who, the what, the when, the where, the why in endless spree.

Wonder questioned only what he would witness.

The actions of adults, he swore were a sickness.

From an innocent child to a sinister soul,

The human race, chaos, they claim to control.

He pondered why parents birthed unwanted kin,

How one soul could be deemed lesser than him?

He mused if men, untethered from prescribed roles,

Would blossom into truer selves, free of societal tolls.

He questioned if sin thrived in the forbidden,

And if the norm was just restriction hidden.

If Praecepta was a box, its walls closing tight,

Forcing lives into molds, a relentless plight.

He questioned why religion dictated the law,

And why society avoided what's raw.

Why problems were hidden in shame's cloak,

While double standards thrived, equality broke.

The lad wondered why a victim was at fault

As though they sought the assault.

How women, creators of life,

Are raised to prioritize their duties as a wife.

Why war was justified, the name of land at stake,

Freedom of speech, a facade, until a stand we make.

Wonder questioned morals, ethics laid bare,

The death of good, a tactic, not rare.

In thought, he mused when society became god,

An everlasting judge, its cruelty seemed odd.

Speculating the possibility, humans wonder too much,

Mending baseless cups, the cracks they clutch.

Wonder questioned the questionable.

Theories and concepts whose examination is ineffable.

In Praecepta, his queries were loathed, for they dared to persist.

For in Praecepta, they reveled in ignorance, an eternal bliss.

I WONDER, I WONDER

What to focus on in the mirror

What to talk about in meetings

"Tell the group 3 fun facts about you!"

Ugh, not again.

I go to my mirror, no reflection.

I wonder why.

*I wonder if I'll ever look at myself the way I want
people to look at me.*

*I wonder if all I will grow to be is a normal person.
Is normal good or is it bad?*

*I wonder when will I be able to forgive myself for
forgiving people.*

I wonder if healing could look chaotic.

*I wonder if we're all sunflowers, if we look where
we can see light and appreciation or do we love
loving what doesn't love us.*

*I wonder why I search for things I can't find in
people who don't exist.*

I wonder if I know as much as I think I do.

I wonder if beauty is more appreciated from afar.

I wonder if the moon is lonely.

I wonder if the loudest people feel heard.

*I wonder why it's really important for me to
understand why.*

*I wonder if each rainbow is the sky remembering
one dear resident that has passed.*

I wonder why people root for belonging.

I wonder if I can look at myself in my mirror again.

I go check it out, it's cracked.

I wonder how superficial my deepest fears are.

I wonder how my skin feels to anyone not judging me.

I wonder if my cats think about the same things as me.

I wonder why love is valuable only because of hate.

I wonder if the reason I can't look in my mirror is that I see too much.

I wonder if wondering is all I do. If finding an answer was never an option.

I wonder if my little self would be proud of me, if my older self is, if I am.

I wonder what it takes to make people speak softly to themselves.

I wonder why love is a superpower.

I glance again at my mirror, it's even more cracked.

I wonder if humor is humor only if someone laughs.

I wonder how green a grass can be before being called fake.

I wonder if colors are just a way for our brain to have fun because it knows that boredom kills.

I wonder why every decision I make feels like the end of the world.

I wonder why I'm so incessant on knowing, being included, including, and receiving reassurance.

I wonder why I fear missing out.

I wonder how I became like this.

I wonder how often do I have to wonder to get an answer.

I wonder how value is measured.

I look at my mirror, it's shattered.

I WONDER

I wonder whether God looks down and cries.

I wonder why the Creator of us all allows racism to exist.

I wonder who could blaspheme God's Creation by taking a child's life.

I wonder what the All-Merciful thinks when his creations destroy one another.

I wonder when we will remember that we were all created "in the image of God".

I wonder how the All-Compassionate sees our lack of compassion for those just like us.

I wonder where on God's earth we can celebrate our differences instead of hating one another.

I wonder whether we can understand that we belong to the land; the land does not belong to us.

I WONDER

I wonder, I wonder, I wonder.

Everyone wonders and everyone does deserve to wonder, I think.

Wondering is a way of escaping reality, well as much as we can, right?

Well, I wonder.

I wonder what peace would look like in a country that was made for peace but has never seen peace before.

Or how I would feel if I woke up tomorrow and there is no hatred, no evil, and no killing of innocent civilians; we all get to live freely, for the most part, at least.

I wonder if people spent money helping the poor and disadvantaged instead of building weapons.

I wonder how children would feel if they were taught that they are all equal no matter what place they come from and that none of them deserve to be killed because their leaders have failed them.

I wonder if all schools accepted both Palestinians and Israelis and taught them about love, peace, and acceptance of the other side from a young age.

If all parents taught their children how to love instead of hate and forgive instead of revenge.

I wonder if there was no difference between us, we respect each other and hear each other and there was finally no injustice.

Well, I wonder.

I wonder if in the near future students can learn about our friendship and our understanding for one another despite everything that has happened in the past.

But as Gandhi said, you have to be the change you wish to see in the world so I hope that I don't have to wonder for much longer.

And instead of wondering, sitting around doing nothing, if me, you, and them work together and teach love, forgiveness, and peace, we can hopefully wonder less.

I WONDER WHY I ALWAYS FEEL LIKE I NEED TO BE THE BEST

I do wonder why I feel the satisfaction of being at my best.

I wonder if it's really me who wants to be at my best. Or are these other people's expectations?

I grew up being the first daughter of the whole family.

Growing up, everyone told me things I wasn't sure about like: you are so smart, you are the prettiest girl, no one can compete with you, you are so quiet and well behaved. You have such a great fashion sense and the hardest one "you are so mature for your age."

There were expectations built. That was who I was supposed to be. Once I stepped out of "being the best" line, and oh my lord, the big wave of disappointment in their eyes. The disbelief on their faces "how dare she."

I do believe the reason we want to be our best all the time is so we feel more superior, more confident, and generally better about ourselves.

However, the pressure of staying in that spot is frustrating. Humans are not robots. None of them have the same feelings. None of them have the same pain tolerance; they are not the same. How can you set one standard for all these human beings?

And even worse, reproach them for living their lives.

I wonder if I always want to be my best or just be a people pleaser.

Maybe the satisfaction I get is from people's approval, the same approval they would take away from you if you have no benefit for them.

I WONDER

I wonder all the time
through the day and through the night
with every step I take
my mind brings me back.
I wonder to escape my pain,
to make it better in my brain.
I imagine all my dreams come true
and wonder if it would happen too.
I wonder if love can change
and hate can take revenge.
I wonder why people lie
even when it makes their loved one's cry.
I wonder if peace exists,
a place without haters and racists.
I wonder what is real and what is fake
and if there is a place where I could be myself.
I wonder why people believe in God
even though reality still hits them with a sword.
I wonder why people sacrifice themselves
in order to save somebody else.
I wonder when will roses lose their smell
and the sky will become blur.
I wonder when my time will come
and what will happen afterward.
I wonder all the time
with every minute and every hour.
I wonder who I am,

I wonder, where do I begin?

Chapter 4 - I Wonder About Today, Tomorrow, the Days After

WONDERING ABOUT THE PRESENT AND THE FUTURE

I wonder about today, its untold stories, guarded secrets, and unturned corners—a chapter yearning to be written with every passing second. Today's whispers and possibilities offer an opportunity to embrace the unknown. Will it be a cascade of laughter or a gentle rain of introspection? Today's fleeting melody molds tomorrow.

I wonder about tomorrow. Tomorrow can be the most anticipated or dreaded day; it all depends on today. And every today is different. Tomorrow hints at promises and potential but also at disappointments and heartbreaks. What tales will it unfurl? What paths will it unveil? Tomorrow dances on the edge of the sunset, a tapestry woven from the threads of dreams and aspirations.

I wonder about the days after. How much have I affected them? Have I already ruined my dreams? Am I dreaming the wrong dream? Is what I'm doing now helping me build my dream? The days after are like distant constellations; they shimmer in an enigmatic dance of destinies and destinations. They hold the weight of dreams yet unknown. The days after are the unwritten epilogue, the sequel to the tales whispered by today and hinted at by tomorrow. I wonder why every day of my life I've been told to do things efficiently and perfectly because my future depends on it. I've been told that all my kindergarten work will affect my future in first grade, and my middle school depends on my elementary school, high school depends on middle school, and college depends on high school. So, I wonder, where does it end? Is life just a boring circle? Always resulting in the same thing. My present depends on my past, my future depends on the present, and my past was once dependent on...and so on and on and on. So I wonder, if life is just a boring circle, why would I fight so hard in the present? Everyone is going to remember the past, but at the same time, very soon, the present will be the past. So, should I just worry all the time? Should the phrase "You only live once" be embraced or banished?

It's a fascinating paradox, isn't it? The tension between making the most of the present and worrying about its fleeting nature can be quite consuming. The present does indeed become the past in the blink of an eye, yet it's where all our actions, decisions, and experiences unfold. Perhaps the essence lies in finding a balance between cherishing the present moment and making choices that align with our future aspirations. But how can we find it? What gives us the power to find it? Isn't it easier to say, "You only live once" and "We'll deal with it later"—is later too late?

In the midst of these swirling thoughts lies the beautiful enigma of life itself. Each passing day, each decision made, is a stroke on the canvas of our existence. Perhaps the resolution to this paradox lies not in a definitive answer but in the journey of discovery. It's about embracing the nuances, the uncertainties, and the ever-shifting balance between seizing the day and planning for tomorrow. The power to navigate this lies within our ability to adapt, learn, and evolve.

I wonder about today, tomorrow, and the day after. I wonder who I will be when the birds come back from migration and what my days will be like. Which books will I have read by then? How many times will I have cried? Will my skin get any better? Will I feel more connected to God? I wonder when it will be my turn To experience, to love, to be fully alive. I wonder when this image I'm drawing of myself will actually be fulfilled. I wonder when I will feel complete. I wonder when I will stop feeling the need to justify myself.

LITTLE LIFE

*In the delicate dance between today, tomorrow,
and the days beyond, I reflect on the canvas of my
existence.*

*Questioning the echoes of today, I ponder if I've
truly savored the tapestry of life or merely stored it
away in the recesses of my mind.*

*Tomorrow, an enigmatic tapestry, unfurls—a blend
of anticipation and trepidation.*

It's the gateway to redemption, a canvas anew.

*Yet, as tomorrows accumulate into the days after,
the allure wanes, transforming interest into
monotony and excitement into an unwelcome
companion named dread.*

*The word "dread" amuses me; when did the eager
child yearning for adulthood find herself dreading
the journey ahead?*

Was it her or the world she navigated?

*Amidst this contemplation, she questions when the
caterpillar of yesteryears metamorphosed into a
mundane moth instead of the promised butterfly.*

*A moth captivated by the alluring glow of
tomorrow, she unwittingly forfeits the present—a
gift overlooked.*

*Reminiscing about the past and orchestrating the
future, she neglects to bask in the simplicity of
laughter and the rhythm of breath.*

*They say life is lived twice—the initial act and the
awakening after realizing the brevity of existence.*

*So, she wonders not just about today, tomorrow,
and the days hence, but most profoundly, about the
day she'll savor life's beauty, slowing down to
admire the butterflies she can yet become.*

I WONDER ABOUT TODAY, TOMORROW, AND THE DAYS AFTER

I WONDER ABOUT TODAY

I wonder whether anything will change today.

I wonder how much bad news today will bring.

I wonder which friends will die, who will lose relatives today.

I wonder if any hostages will get to go home to their families today.

I wonder how to celebrate a holiday about Jewish survival from enemies trying to destroy us while so many enemies still want to destroy us.

I wonder if the light can shine through the darkness today.

I WONDER ABOUT TOMORROW

I wonder if I could wake up and it would all be a horrific nightmare.

I wonder if tomorrow will be the day that we can start to feel everyone's pain.

I wonder if tomorrow our leaders will lead instead of pointing fingers and hiding.

I wonder if it's possible to root out an ideology using weapons, and if the process will do more harm than good.

I wonder if tomorrow the world can be a little freer, with a little less hatred, and a little more understanding and love.

I WONDER ABOUT THE DAYS AFTER

I wonder if I will see my friends face to face one day.

I wonder how many will be left for me to meet.

47

I wonder how we can rebuild together.

I wonder when those with the money, the weapons, and the power will look past today and tomorrow and think about the Days After.

I wonder if I will wonder the same things in the Days After.

I WONDER ABOUT TODAY, TOMORROW, AND THE DAY AFTER

I wonder about every day all day. I wonder about tomorrow and the day after tomorrow.

I wonder about my future and if I'll even have a future.

I wonder what my insecurities are gonna be next week.

I wonder if I'll stop criticizing myself in the near future—whether by my looks, my personality, the way I talk, or the way I walk.

But I'm never going to stop, right? Because it's something disgusting that I always tend to do, and I hate it so much. I hate it because it makes me hate myself.

I wonder why it's mostly girls that feel that way.

I wonder if people will ever stop saying beauty is from within but judge you if you are not thin.

I wonder when my body will be enough for me.

I wonder when I will be able to stop comparing myself with others.

I wonder when this voice inside of me will go away.

I wonder if society will change.

I wonder if the next generation will do better and start realizing the gravity of this nightmare.

WONDER ABOUT TODAY, TOMORROW, AND THE DAY AFTER

When you come home at the end of the day,

after a long, long day, and lay down,

then, by all means, wonder about tomorrow,

whether full of happiness or sorrow.

Consider your actions for the next week;

progress, like a house, is built brick by brick.

Wonder—paint the greatest picture in your mind;

make sure you leave no detail behind.

Happiness, grief, joy, whatever you may feel,

wondering will make your heart heal.

Just wander around in your mind for a minute or two;

process your thoughts; every day, I do it too.

Wonder about the following days, wander around—

don't be shy, walk, run, get off the ground.

Build your own 'Wonderland'—follow the rabbit;

be your own Alice, I can promise you, it's a great habit.

In your wonderland, you can never be late;

let it be a sanctuary, free of hate.

Imagine whatever you wish; drink from the bottle— get smaller;

do whatever you want; eat the cake—grow taller.

They say, 'Be the change you want to see';
start in your mind, be you, get free.
Be the king of the hill, run to be president;
paint a better world, don't be hesitant.

Don't let them touch the beaver or the snark,
or go hunt them both before it gets dark.
Smile so kindly back at the cat,
or buy, from its friend, a brand new hat.

But when you come home at the end of the day,
sit for a moment and imagine a world a bit less
gray.
And in the morning after—stop wondering, until
the next sunset;
start doing, paint the better picture, be the king—
this you will not regret.

I WONDER ABOUT TODAY, TOMORROW, AND THE DAY AFTER

I WONDER ABOUT TODAY

I wonder: has anything changed in the last few
months?

I wonder: are things better or worse?

I wonder how we can celebrate birthdays and
holidays when people are still living through a
nightmare.

I wonder if any of the hostages are still alive.

I wonder if we have hit rock bottom yet.

50

I wonder how it's possible to have fruits and vegetables waiting to be picked while a population is starving next door.

I wonder why countries criticize Israel and then close their doors to Gazans.

I WONDER ABOUT TOMORROW

I wonder if tomorrow will be worse.

I wonder if any families will be reunited tomorrow.

I wonder if tomorrow any "leaders" will be held accountable.

I wonder if all those who claim to care would actually help those in need.

I wonder if tomorrow we will lose this feeling of unity.

I wonder if we've reached tomorrow yet.

I WONDER ABOUT THE DAY AFTER

I wonder how you can go to war without thinking of the day after.

I wonder what we can do to prepare for the day after.

I wonder how to believe that the day after will be better.

I wonder if our path is linear or circular.

I wonder how to talk about "the day after" with people who can't even imagine "tomorrow."

Chapter 5 - Fear, Stress, and Hope

WRITING OUR EMOTIONS DURING WAR

The Feeling You Only Hear About

60 days have passed since the war began. Sixty days in which I feel empty. Sixty days of an emotional roller coaster that doesn't have a rising trend. All I hear around me is the word "death." The whispers at school were all gossip and teenage drama, but now it's all about the horrors, the murders, the unspeakable. Social media is covered in videos of people's last phone calls to their loved ones. I see posts from people describing what they saw when the Hamas terrorists broke into their homes: how they beat, kicked, and burned their loved ones and beheaded them in front of their eyes. I break down every time I see an influencer who has changed my life support and raise money for the people trying to murder me, my friends, and my family merely because I am Jewish.

Our television is constantly tuned to the news channel these days. I don't know what I want to see; perhaps it's the hope of catching some good news for a change. I saw live footage on the news of Hamas terrorists, pro-camera, throwing grenades at children, toddlers, and babies as they screamed for their parents. But their parents won't come; they are already dead on the kitchen floor.

I've tried hundreds of times to think why. Why would people walk around the street whistling and shooting people? Why would anyone take a life, someone they don't know, a complete stranger, because of the sole fact that they are Jewish? I thought about it for a while and remembered one of the worst things that occurred in history: The Holocaust. At school, on Holocaust Memorial Day, survivors tell us how they had to live for days in a hole they had dug themselves, without food, without water, without air. They told how the Nazis broke into their homes and beat and executed their father, raped their mother, and burned their siblings alive. One of the Holocaust survivors came to my school and told us how the Nazis took him and about two hundred other children and babies to a small house. They locked them in there and set it on fire. He heard them laughing outside without caring at all as he struggled to breathe, fighting for every bit of oxygen. Luckily, he survived; unfortunately, his two other siblings died in the fire. I always think about how they felt, how incredibly scared they were, how helpless, confused, and extremely frightened. However, I could never really understand it. I was not there; my house wasn't broken into; no one came and murdered my family in cold blood.

One Saturday, I was doing my homework and listening to music. It was a sunny day; the weather was perfect. Suddenly, I heard a notification on my cell phone. I opened it and felt my skin burning; it was as if a million little needles had pricked me all at once. I had goosebumps. I was cold - the color had drained from my face - I looked like I had seen a ghost, but I didn't. I saw worse. I saw that three new articles had been published. One was about how a Jewish man was murdered in California after an altercation at an Israeli-Palestine protest. The second was a photo of a Jewish man's front door in Germany with a swastika spray-painted on it. The third was the worst of all: more photos showing hundreds of gravestones in a Jewish cemetery in Brooklyn with swastikas spray-painted in red.

I found it hard to breathe; I couldn't breathe. A painful shiver went through my body. It was at that moment when I realized that this war is not between Israel and Palestine but worldwide. People in Germany, France, and even in the United States, friendly countries, want me dead. But why? They do not know me, and I do not know them. It was then that I understood a little of the fear that the Jews had to go through during the Holocaust. The unimaginable fear of existing. I understood the fear when you hear a faint noise outside that makes you jump, thinking they are outside, ready to break in and take your last breath. I felt the horrible feeling of something I only heard of in stories.

Will this war turn into another Holocaust? It already feels like it. Jews are being tortured, raped, abused, beheaded, burned alive, drowned, electrocuted until their last breath, and swastikas sprayed on doors and tombstones.

Will I have to be walked with my eyes closed and my hands tied to a place that was built specifically to kill me? Will I have to hide my three-year-old sister underground with me so they won't find us? Will I have to change my identity to keep my life?

Stress

I find myself saying I'm stressed most of the time. It's a word I use to express myself whenever anyone asks me how I'm feeling, and I don't feel like dealing with my emotions. However, during the last few weeks, I learned what stress really means to me. Stress is a heart that's aching, crying out, and dying. It's the fear of failure, but there is still no urge to be productive. It's being overwhelmed and under a lot of pressure but still not knowing what to do – how to handle it. It's not being able to sleep because you're overthinking every little thing that comes into your mind. It's a pain that is so hard to get rid of and seems to linger around. I'm stressing over things no teenager or no one ever should stress over.

I'm stressing over things like wanting to do my absolute best and never stop because I'm alive and in good health. I can't take being alive for granted because I have the chance to achieve my dreams, unlike those many children who have been unfortunately killed before their dreams could be fulfilled. They each had dreams and goals, some of which might have been better than mine. I will never know. I can't stop thinking how they might have become something big in this evil world and how we let these children down and made them face consequences they weren't involved in. I can't stop stressing over the fact that I can't fail them again in the future, that is, if they are able to survive.

I stress so much over the fact that my parents can get fired for saying anything that expresses how they really feel, and I stress because my sister might get kicked out of college because of her nationality and identity. I stress over losing one of my friends who's fighting for their lives right now. I stress because of my worry and pain that control my thoughts all day, every day.

I stress, I stress, I stress.

I'm stuck between my thoughts and reality. I'm lost. I'm trying to find a way out, but yet every door seems closed, and I'm suffocating, and I'm scared. So scared.

I didn't choose where to be born. I didn't choose what nationality my ancestors should have. I didn't choose this life, but yet I'm still handling it. Although it's killing me from the inside seeing my people suffer, I wouldn't trade my nationality for the world because my people have faith - my people know life. My people will never give up.

CHANGE

People sometimes close their eyes to ignore what
they have seen.

Hearts get tired of explaining thoughts and what
spoken words mean.

Judging and overthinking kill pleasure and cause
bodies to lean.

Stop the suffering because it leads to losing
everything that once had been.

Get up! Get alive! Days run so fast, adding to the
number of years of age.

Creatures are different, but all of them live
together in the same cage.

It is the wild wide world that separates members by
the written page,

*Titling them with names of countries and
nationalities, from familiar to strange.*

*It tires the mind until brains are updated to break
darkness by the light of the sun,*

*To cancel limits, pain, and hate and spread love
everywhere, joy, and fun.*

*To love each other, help, realize dreams, work
hard, and act all as one.*

*To close all the files of fight, pain, and war and
throw them away with a sign of DONE.*

THE DEVIL IN THE COSTUME OF AN ANGEL

If you ask me whom I see,
I would tell you: your enemy.
They hide behind a mask
And laugh in the dark.
They show neither mercy nor regret;
It is who they are, don't act ignorant.

They run from reality
But hide inside society.
They film their inhumanity,
Which proves their cruelty.
You should fear,
Because they are here.

It is not a game nor make-believe;
It's just our life that could come to its end.
We call them the devils,
But others think of them as angels.
They claim they are innocent,
But use violence as their privilege.

CONNECTING THROUGH PAIN

Two years ago, during the summer, I read "Colourless Tsukuru Tazaki and His Years of Pilgrimage," a novel by my favorite author, Haruki Murakami. This one quote proposed a unique idea that hasn't left my mind since then: "One heart is not connected to another through harmony alone. They are, instead, linked deeply through their wounds. Pain linked to pain, fragility to fragility. There is no silence without a cry of grief, no forgiveness without bloodshed, no acceptance without a passage through acute loss. That is what lies at the root of true harmony."

This quote fascinated me when I read it for the first time. I love it since it challenges the romanticized notion of connection. It suggests that the truest bonds are forged not in moments of unfettered happiness but in the crucible of pain. Pain, in its myriad forms, becomes the unexpected bridge between souls.

Søren Kierkegaard, a Danish philosopher, is well-known for his concept of "inwardness," the deep, introspective understanding of oneself and one's place in the world. Inwardness involves confronting and embracing our pain and suffering, recognizing them as integral to our existence. Through this inward journey, we develop a deeper understanding of ourselves and, consequently, a greater capacity to connect with others.

I believe that, especially at such dark times when we often find ourselves left alone with our sorrows and sadness, it's essential for us to embrace our inwardness and acknowledge our pain. It requires courage to face our own suffering and to share it with others. Yet, it is precisely this act of sharing that transforms our pain from a source of isolation and alienation into a source of connection. In my opinion, sadness is the most powerful human emotion, so powerful that it can connect scattered hearts filled with hatred. Whenever we encounter another's pain and sorrow, we recognize a reflection of our own experiences. This recognition doesn't diminish our individual suffering but rather situates it within a broader, shared narrative.

This understanding can be quite comforting, right? It shifts our perspective from isolation to interconnectedness. Our suffering, while deeply personal, becomes a bridge to others.

THE FALLEN ANGEL

They say that the fallen angel sowed evil on earth once he landed.

They say they pray to the Lord, asking the fallen angel about the lost paradise that Milton wrote about.

But weren't people created in the likeness of angels? Yes, but why do people choose the fallen angel's side?

Why did my brother try to kill me while I was asleep? Why did my brother, with whom I wanted eternal peace, stab me in the back?

I'm sorry, brother, that you are suffering for your choice; I'm just trying to protect myself.

I'm sorry that because of your choice, my other brothers got closer to God.

But I'm not sorry for protecting the promised people of my God.

And I am not sorry for protecting God's promised land for His chosen people.

Angel, I'm sorry that the fallen angel set you up.

Angel, has your soul found the lost paradise that Milton wrote about?

And I'm sorry I couldn't protect you from that fallen angel who stabbed your back.

Angel, I'm sorry I couldn't protect you on that bloody morning.

But now, I finally know that you found that lost paradise.

Finding The Hope: Hatikva Market

I love walking through the Shuk on a Friday morning at the Tiqva market. The sounds—vendors screaming, the karaoke at the hummus stand, all the languages: Hebrew, Arabic, Amharic, Russian, Tigray, English, Persian, all intertwined, the smells of the spices and freshly baked bread, the bright colors of the fruits and vegetables—it all feels so alive.

After October 7th, it wasn't alive. People came to get the necessities, but life was gone. There were fewer people out and about, and those who went out, lacked energy. No one was singing, and even the vendors hawking their goods were more subdued as if they knew that the price of a pineapple or a cluster of grapes simply didn't matter as much. People looked shell-shocked, like human zombies. I didn't see much fear—if there's a demographic in Israel who doesn't have fear, it's the people who live in my neighborhood. We knew life would go on; it must. But the joy, and even the vitality, was missing.

It took weeks, maybe months, to come back. Probably the biggest factor was the hostage exchange when families were reunited. Those who had prayed and hoped but were afraid to dream could finally sleep at night. But slowly, gradually, you can feel the tempo coming back. When I walked the streets of Shuk Hatikva on Friday, three days before we'd leave for the US, there was singing again. I could barely walk through the marketplace, squeezing by the Eritrean families, the Chinese workers on their bicycles, old men in their wheelchairs and motorized vehicles, and young children being pushed in strollers. The sounds, smells, and colors are back—the Shuk is again alive. Almost like it was before.

Almost. But not quite. It's still not the same. It can't be. We still see the posters of our missing people, of the hostages staring back at us, challenging us to bring them home. We carry that burden around our necks, on our shirts, and in our heart. Until every last person comes home, or much worse, is found to be dead already, things can never be the same. It's hard to describe the

Israeli feeling about hostages, but it's completely foreign to the American part of my identity. I remember when I first moved to the country and Gilad Shalit was being held by Hamas. One captured soldier captured the heart of an entire nation, and we had endless prayer vigils and political protests for him until, eventually, 1,000 prisoners were released to bring him home. Now, multiply that 100-fold. The math won't compute.

We're at six months now. Six months of this bloody, awful war. The newspapers mark this grim milestone somberly. It seems unthinkable that we've been at this for half a year—yet it also feels like it's been far longer than that. When and how might it end? It seems like no one knows the answer. It feels like there's no clear strategy. The end goal is to eradicate Hamas, but how and what comes next. And where do our missing loved ones fit into all of that?

I think about my friends in Gaza too. At the beginning of the war, we talked almost daily. Implausibly, war galvanized our friendship. Some days, it felt like they were the only ones I could talk to—because amidst all of the polarization, knowing that we could have empathy for one another was a lifeline. But now I feel them slipping away, falling deeper into depression, losing hope. They've lost family, friends, homes, and livelihoods—their past uprooted, their present shredded, their future in limbo. Some haven't been heard from in weeks; I fear the worst.

I wish I could bring them here—to show them around the Hatikva market, show them the strength of a nation that, no matter what happens, always picks itself up off the floor and keeps going because truly we have no other choice, no other home. A place that has flaws and wrinkles but still manages to encompass Jews, Muslims, Christians, Druze, and people of all different backgrounds. Hatikva means hope, and I wish I could give them hope. I wish I had hope to share. Instead, I pick out the vegetables and head home to help my wife prepare for Shabbat. For now, we survive. Hope will come eventually, or so I hope.

WORTH LIVING

I am at home.

I don't really know if I have enough words to explain or describe; I don't even know why I'm writing this, and I'm not sure I'll be able to touch many hearts with the alphabet soup I'm about to spit out. I also don't know if I should be writing this, nor if my grammar is correct or if I will be able to stop lying about the "I don't know" part.

I'm exhausted. I have two more months left of school and too much exam stress to deal with. I'm typing these letters while I'm sitting at home on the couch, my legs crossed on top of each other, our TV playing in the background. My grandma is watching the news on Al Jazeera, and my grandpa is sleeping. I'm at home. I just came back from school. I go to the Hand In Hand school in Jerusalem. It's a school for both Palestinians and Israelis. It's also the only place where I feel I can speak comfortably and freely.

I'm at home. I'm tired. I won't use any complex language, and I will try to be as straightforward as possible. People, humans like me, like you, like us, are being killed, tortured, starved, and forced to flee their houses due to them being bombed right now. I invite you all to take one second and try to put yourself in their place. Please close your eyes for one second. Imagine losing everything you've ever loved and known in seconds. Did you feel anything?

I want to finish school and go to university, and I want to become the best doctor in town or the best diplomat; I still haven't decided, and that's another story, but both careers are ones that I dream of pursuing in the hope that I will be able to help my people in the future.

I want to build a house, start a professional soccer team for little girls, read as many books as possible, and travel around the world. I also want to burn down the stupid system and the way it works. I love my family, friends, people, and nation. Love is another huge story. The point is, I do have dreams and goals that I love and care about and many things to lose. Because that's how I'm built, and that's how everyone is built. And most of us are privileged, somehow. The problem is that each of us uses our privilege differently. My people in Gaza are also humans. Every single one of them has their priorities, ambitions, things, and people they love. They have dreams - feelings and emotions like you and me.

See, it's also quite difficult and very exhausting that I must explain to people how and why we Palestinians are also humans who deserve to live safely and freely and be granted basic rights. I apologize, I did not intend to make this all about me. However, that's my indirect answer to everyone afraid to speak up and go down to the streets and to everyone who constantly nags me to step aside, step back, stay safe, and not participate in this misguided game called politics.

I'm angry. I'm sad. But do you know what feeling is bothering me the most? Helplessness. People, my people, my brothers and sisters, Palestinians just like me, in Gaza, are being tortured, and I cannot do anything about it. I'm writing. I'm sharing. I'm posting. And I'm going down to the streets every single time I can. I'm meeting people worldwide and teaching them about the problem. But yet, I feel like I'm not doing anything about it. Because I'm not a system. I'm Yara. Just Yara.

I don't intend to convince you all to speak up. I'm just writing because I cannot breathe - writing is my therapy. And because I care. I may be an emotional teenager in the eyes of many adults, but I still choose to write.

Nothing about our lives is normal, but we normalize everything. Because facing our daily reality is way too scary. I think it's a coping mechanism that most of us tend to use, so whenever they ask us how we are, we say we are better and getting used to it.

But then again, what exactly is there to get used to when we are not the ones physically getting hurt and forced to leave our houses?

I mean, of course, we are hurt mentally, and our hearts ache for them, but we always manage to distract ourselves somehow. But how can they distract themselves from the torture they are living in?

Writing this is too heavy mentally, and my heart is breaking. I don't know how I'm supposed to end this. I just hope there is a good ending.

And that was me. Now, let's take another second to imagine what the families in Gaza are currently going through.

As the Palestinian poet Mahmoud Darwish once said: "We have on this land that which makes life worth living."

But really, is there something that still makes life worth living?

Chapter 6 - Family

GIVING THANKS FOR OUR FAMILY

DAFFODIL

This is a very special poem that I wrote about my special sister who had special needs and whom I lost three years ago. Her name was Narjes. Narjes is the Arabic name for the rose daffodil.

Does modern life give technology the right to change someone's emotions?

Categorizing them into groups and names by the lie of globalization,

Convincing them that people are different, peoples of more than a nation,

Which lets them live behind the screens until they turn with no appreciation,

Killing the union of belonging and fighting to get it back through organization,

Struggling not to lose containing the other through the coming generation.

God created the universe, putting His beauty and specialty into His creation,

And made all people equal and free, but differences are found in education.

He prefers educated scientists who will treat the sickness and passion,

Giving them the mind to search for any information,

Teaching people about the beauty of special people with syndromes' situations,

And raising the feeling of care and love for them with consideration.

*They are "The Special Ones" that have ever been
found in the whole creation.*

*In one spot of the globe, there was a garden in an
unknown location.*

*Roses grew with a lavender smell, and one different
rose got attention.*

*It was a daffodil in the lavender field, a foreign
rose of creation.*

*The flowers went far from jealousy and captured it
in the prison of isolation,*

*Till the farmer came and defined its beauty that
decorated the location,*

*Watered it carefully, and took care of it with a fear
of coming pollution.*

*It was strange to feel like the daffodil was calling
for any communication.*

*The wise farmer got the gift from God as the
specialty in differentiation,*

*And was proud that he was chosen to get God's
preferred treatment,*

*To send him this daffodil that is not found in any
other location,*

*Decorating his simple hut to be a great castle in a
world of imagination.*

*Teaching each one of us the meaning of being
thankful with appreciation,*

*And being aware to value even the smallest thing
that may cause a revolution,*

*That may change life for the better and give the
real meaning of "pure relation."*

*Gave them the power to study the brain, looking
and searching for any information.*

TO MY MOTHER

To the mothers of the world,

To the mothers young and old,

To the mothers of daughters and those of sons,

*To the mothers who birthed their children and
those who took them in,*

*To the mothers who outlived their babies and those
who said goodbye,*

*To the mothers who were forced to be mothers and
those who were unable to be mothers,*

To the mothers of the world, I am deeply sorry.

I can't pinpoint the exact moment, but somewhere over the years as I grew up, my mother became more than just my source of life. The very entity I clung to for dear life, every scraped knee, tangled hair, and broken heart—she was created to mend me back together, to love me. She was a goddess, beautiful, erect, and extraordinary. But somewhere over the years, she became human in my eyes. She had faults and fleeting moments of anger. Her tongue was like the sea, sharp yet a calm remedy. She was a mother, but she also had a mother and was still a daughter just like me. Her very existence made me wonder about motherhood. How had it shaped her life? Or how had it taken it from her?

I look at our precious time together and regret not acknowledging the fact that she was living life for the very first time too. She was told to be Wonder Woman; she barely got to be a woman. A woman confusing surviving with living.

My own mother made me never want to be a mother. Oh, how she sacrificed herself like a lamb for slaughter, her first choice always being the last chosen, manicures she could afford were given to her little girls, every extra penny spent on shoes size four. Every restaurant visit is accompanied by "I'll eat whatever you don't." I didn't think to leave her food. I should have. I should have said sorry. You were a punching bag, bloody and bruised, and my little fists with weak throws let out all the anger on you.

I learned from my mother the skills it takes to be a mother. Motherhood was a job not for the weak. Motherhood was losing yourself, who you are, no longer making time for things you like to do. Motherhood was selflessness, wisdom, and determination. Motherhood was the concern your kids would turn out okay, secret hopefulness, that your kids would change the world.

Motherhood was not lightness and sweetness. Motherhood was rage and roller coasters and life. Motherhood was creating a daughter with your personality and a son who has your eyes. Motherhood was falling so deeply in love and being so excruciatingly loved. Motherhood was feeling unconditional love. Motherhood changes you; everything you've ever known is no

69

longer relevant. Their first steps are also yours. Motherhood is so extremely fragile. Though if you do it right, however you may interpret that, you may wind up having a daughter who loves half as much as I love my mommy.

I wonder if today, there are millions of children being mothered by mothers who didn't want them. I wonder if tomorrow we could live in a world where motherhood was mended, the cracks filled and cups overflowing. If mothers wouldn't be shamed for feeling overwhelmed, holding weights on their shoulders society can take off. I wonder about the days after when I shall be a mother and have a daughter. Introduce her to all my favorite books, show her the place that holds my best memories and create new core memories with her. I wonder how motherhood will change me.

My mother has all the answers, or she once did. I grew up; time is a bittersweet factor of childhood. You change so rapidly, but then again, some things never change. Nature vs. nurture. You nurtured me in a world where I had to grow up. You nurtured me to be a good person, to be a voice for those in need. To smile and make jokes; life flies by. But I think it's in my nature to love you. It's in my nature to ask you all my questions. Though I am old enough to know sometimes you are just lost as me. That's beauty. I asked you in the beginning of the war and then again half a year later who is most broken from this living hell. Without a moment of thought, you turned to me and held my gaze and said mothers. Mothers who have lost their children. I didn't quite understand, then I did. Mothers live for their children. Life is empty without them.

To the mothers of Israeli souls and to the mothers of Palestinian souls who have gone to a better place, I am sorry. To all the mothers, who held limp stillborns in their fragile arms. To the mothers who lost children to a bottle or pill. To the mothers who found their kids with horizontal lines across their body. To the ones who were too late and couldn't save their sons and daughters. To the mothers who feel overwhelmed with the responsibility, undervalued for all the effort they put in. To the mothers who survived civil wars, genocide and terror only to come out of it all alone. You should be proud of all you did. For the paths you carved for your babies, the very road you never could take. I am sorry to all the mothers living without their other halves and all the kids who feel a gaping hole in their heart.

My mother crawled through life so I may sprint. For every steep mountain you climb, I run across a hill; every wild sea, I float in clear water; and in every dangerous jungle, I may walk freely among the trees. To the little girl my mother used to be, I hope you're happy. A ballerina, famous actress, an astronaut, you are not, but in my world, you are. When I grow up, I want to be someone you are so proud of, so that your eyes gleam with tears, your heart bursting out of your chest at the sight of me. No matter the path I choose, in every single one, every world, every universe, every version of time, I hope to be loved at least half as much as you loved me. You took the bar of how to be loved and raised it to the sky. To my dear mother, your mini-me, your left extension, always to the moon and back. When you depart from this world, may you look at your life and feel fulfilled, may you be at peace with your time, and greet death like a friend. But never actually leave me. Wait for me on the other side too. You promise, mama?

I am my mother's daughter. She dances with the wind and I try to tame it. She ignites the fire and I maintain it. Dear mother, never stop being who you are because my personality is a reflection of yours with my own personal tweaks. You see me, see deep into my soul and dissect every reason in order to let me heal. You're the one who sees the battles within and fights them like David and Goliath, fearlessly no matter the size.

In another life, I would like to come back as my mother's mother. To braid her curls and kiss her goodnight. Read her to sleep like the 1001 Arabian nights. To hold her tight in my arms, gaze into her hazel eyes, to reassure her she shall only be a mother if she wants to be. To the children who never felt a mother's love, I truly, truly am sorry. Be the mothers you wished you had. Or don't bring children into this world that is crumbling, the world is ablaze and the flames have reached the innocent.

HOPE

To all the people that I know and have met during my life chapter.

A message of love I want to send for being a daughter, sister, wife, and a mother.

First, I want to say "alhamdulillah" for being me as I am and thanks to God for creating me in a good shape and complete picture.

I look to the skies so thankful for all the blessings that I get from You, Lord, calling, praying, thanking and asking that me to you become closer.

You always balance my life, even when I have the greatest worries and heaviest responsibilities, but you give me the wisdom to struggle and the power of a fighter.

It is the uniqueness of feeling others' pain, being the helping hand for who need it and seeing all people as they are the same and not " judging the book by its cover"

I have lost precious ones in my life, I cried, got frustrated then realized Your generosity for choosing me to be the warrior and the winner.

For getting the best dad that can be found on earth, and a very special sister.

I got the honor to serve and take care of them, like You telling me to do the mission and go up higher.

To get the highest human degrees of being an obedient daughter, good sister and successful fighter.

The prize is getting my mom's wishes to God to keep and protect me from dangers by calling God " الله يرضى عليكي " my daughter.

The best winning of gold medal is getting a unique or even the best man on earth ever.

*A loving, caring, sharing, and supporting husband
and an amazing role model father*

*That helps me raise four lovely roses in our garden
of life by containing me and them and holding us
together.*

*To face the rudeness of life and fight for the place
to which we belong forever:*

*The holy place of The Holy Land that lives for so
many years and was attacked by dangerous minds
of haters.*

*Who want to convince people to live in groups,
split them from the tree of union, humanity and
cancel the meaning of lives if all as one matter.*

*Hey you! You are totally wrong! All as one, and
one cares for all, that is the point that we must
raise the generations at, so do not create a gap and
make it wider.*

*I was born as a Muslim Arab, so I practice Islam
and speak Arabic and live in the holy land; my best
friends are Christians, Druze, Jewish with a
pleasure.*

*Stop mixing cards together, acting the worst way
and trying to show that things are different by
judging the book cover.*

*Your tries will not be taken anymore because we
are realizing that our differences create an unique
figure.*

*You will not cancel me if I am the other, and I will
not let you live the saying "the other is me", no it is
a mistake dear hater.*

*Me is me, you must get this and respect me as I do
by taking that you are the other and I do accept
and respect with pleasure.*

Chapter 7 - Spreading Our Wings

WRITING TO TAKE OFF AND FLY AWAY

BUTTERFLY

I wonder if I were a butterfly,

I wonder if I could just flap my wings and fly above it all,

Live among the flowers,

A tranquil life of bright colors and pleasant smells.

I wonder if I'd see the changes,

Notice fewer trees and more smog,

See the people scurrying by, with no time for roses.

I wonder if I'd wonder,

Why those weird creatures who walk on two limbs can't get along.

Butterflies don't fight—why do the humans? Don't they want to be happy?

I wonder if I'd give up,

Just flap those wings and move on,

Find a happier place to spend my days, free from worries and strife.

The Ember Bird

It was a cold morning in November,

As much as I can recall, remember,

When in the cold yet pleasant land of home,

He stood after sleepless night, alone.

He saw a bird, in reddish color, ember.

As a hunter jumped, he, when the bird had spoken,

But then a silence followed, even when he asked,
"What is thy name?" It remained unbroken.

After an eternity of silence, the bird opened her
mouth and thus it read:

Only one word, and no more, her lips said, "Dead."

"Dead?" inquired the man, with eyes wide open.

The bird proceeded again to whisper, but one
word, "Dead."

In obvious surprise and utter confusion, he shook
his head.

"Please, noble bird," then he cried,

"To help I yearn, but first tell me who has died."

But as before, not a word she uttered, not even a
shred.

To his home he started to return, but the bird had
followed,

Into his room, beyond the door, into the house that
was hollowed.

Softer became her heart, and so deeply help she
wanted,

That the bird flew faster into the room, after the
door, almost as if she was haunted.

And then she spoke, with painful eyes, her tears she
swallowed.

"The hunter, amidst the night, came with a rifle and
aimed,

For he had us by surprise, we did not flee, he was
highly skilled and trained,"

So cried the ember bird. "All my family, his rifle
took,"

Then the man said, "He will not get off the hook,"

Till the night they stayed in the house and at last
said, "Your house, bird, shall be reclaimed."

As the morning came, with fierce faces of warriors,
they went

To the former nest they traveled for hours until
midway they put up a tent.

At last they came. With a cracked voice stated the
bird, "O, my nest burned to the ground,

Who is the devil that would commit those
atrocities? O, my nest, just look around."

For eternity they stayed there, lying, the ember
bird's family. They did lament.

To the vicious hunter's house, then they traveled,
an old house of stone and wood,

In the middle of the room, a young man with a
fouled face stood.

At the first moment, when they could, into the house
they glanced,

77

And a terrible sight of countless cages was seen.
"We must plan to ever get advanced,"

Fall back is what they did, and for the rest of the
night they planned the best they could.

When the sun rose and the moon went down, in the
dimly lighted foggy morning,

The man and the ember bird went as planned, to
attack without warning.

The man threw a rock at the window while the bird
entered and flew to the cages.

As determined as ever, could be maneuvered the
bird, yet there were a few changes.

But lo and behold, the murderous hunter began his
run, what an odious turning!

All the cages were freed that morning. As the last
one opened, a horrible scream.

And in one moment, two shots, there was no longer
a team.

The hunter laughed, and shots were heard, but
indeed who got hurt?

All were free, but it was not a happy morning.
None were happy, not even the ember bird.

Although the bird got her revenge, she mourned for
hours - what kind of a dream?!

In the end of the event, two bodies were lying on
the old wooden house's floor.

One of the hunter and the other of the kind man,
the team's core.

Only deafening silence was heard, no one got up,
no one got down.

And so the birds of the cages and the ember one left the town.

Years after, when the ember bird told her story, she always concluded, "Only him I adore."

Years after, when questions were asked, only then the world knew about the hunter—though the topic was tender.

At first no one cared and no one mourned, though the bird tried to move, she did flounder.

But then as the years went by, and people started to see,

Who indeed was the public's enemy.

But as people realized and wanted to hear—one last shot to the heart of the bird of ember.

LILIES AND DOVES, PAWNS OF WAR

I am a lily, and you are a dove,
Destined to blossom and destined to fly above.

Yet, how can I blossom with no water and light,
And how can you soar, wings clipped, in this fight?

A gilded cage they craft, illusions so fine,
Yet beneath the gold, it's metal that binds.

They plucked my petals, stripped your feathers too,
Chained us with threads unseen, an insidious brew.

Your actions, brushstrokes, objectify our youth,
Assigned us names, played us as pawns, a ruthless
truth.

They asked, 'What will you be when grown up,
pray?'
Yet long before eighteen, life's road grows dim and
gray.

In war's cruel dance, where innocence is the cost,
Children, once lilies and doves, too often are lost.

Once a lily, once a dove in skies above,
Now a black rose, a reflection of a raven's love.

Take that as you please, but we beg you to see,

The lilies and doves you once used to be.

We seek not pity or pledges hollow,
But a plea to cease this game, compassion to
follow.

We were lilies and doves, innocent and free,
Cease before more innocence fades, let children be.

A BOX OF MYSTERY

I was flying high when I found myself in a white fog,

It was obstructing me and pulling me down.

I stood up and grabbed it. It disappeared from the sky.

My hands were very slow but too fast for me to comprehend,

Everything was scattered but all gathered at once,

It was all smooth but made my hands bloody from its severity,

And he disguised himself.

The first thing I picked up was an audio tape.

I pressed the play button and it was very loud,

But it was the calmest and softest sound I had ever heard.

"If you're listening to this tape, congratulations, you're me, and I'm you.

Not really, but we are very much alike,

If not, you wouldn't be able to find me.

Can you make the box our little secret?

You may not remember me but your soul will;

This box was made during a year I assume you want to forget forever,

But you did your best to store it and you did not want to preserve it but you did.

I know you, as I mentioned before, it's both a blessing and a curse.

Let's take a tour of what I had in mind when I left
you this box,

What I decided to keep, and what you see in your
hands.

Now, this tape is what can remind you of what
happened in the year

You decided to create this box, that year was what
no one expected,

And most of the memories from it make it clear that
it was from the past.

In one way or another, it affected everything.

It was hurtful, and its events were unexpected.

These objects that you see now are the chosen
ones.

The second thing I want you to look at is that doll.

The same doll that accompanied you throughout
the year and everything you went through.

It was always her,

The only one who always accompanied you, heard
all your problems,

Saw you in all your days and all your feelings, and
went through everything with you.

If only we could revive her,

She would have talked about you more than you
talk about yourself.

You'd think she's in love with you.

She would talk about everything you went through,

And she would get rid of those who hurt you,

And she would have "given you your rights."

She will talk about the reflection of the tears that
flowed from your eyes.

83

How her eyes witnessed both moments of
overwhelming joy

And complete disappointment,

Overwhelming hope, overwhelming fear,

Overwhelming confidence, and suppressed
sadness.

She would have spoken of your night "explosions":

The walls of your room being filled with music,

Hoping that your anger will be healed,

You healing your wounds while the night passes,
the very black and rigid and night passing.

There is nothing wrong with remembering what
you went through.

That is life, and if not now, then surely someday
you will be proud of me, of you, of us.

Third is that pen,

It is the same pen in which you wrote your dreams
and carried everywhere.

It made everyone you knew laugh.

That what you carry with you is just a pen and it
made you laugh.

They thought it was just a pen,

But like the reason why you carried it, like your
dreams,

You preferred to keep it to yourself.

It is easier to believe that our secrets are in a safe
place with us.

Your pen was your mouth.

All your writings were your consolations.

Sitting with yourself and letting it lead you,

You felt like that pen was your second mouth,

And sometimes because of the excess of words in your mouth,

You became unable to speak and became stifled.

Suddenly, you release what is in your mind and it rages,

Trying to find logic in the events in your brain

To translate the storm into a dance of ink on the surface

Of paper and increase the number of your stocks.

The fourth thing is the sea,

The same place you used to run to when you needed peace and quiet.

Its waters were your escape and your savior.

Its stillness, as if it could not turn into your killer, your destroyer, and your exhauster, dazzled you.

You loved what you did not understand, and you did not understand the sea,

And I was hoping that you'd never understand it.

You liked that it was a mystery and mysteries are what kept you alive.

You liked that it was layered and when everyone brags about visiting the sea you knew that,

In fact, they had not visited anything in the sea and did not know its guts.

Did not know what was inside it, but fully believed that they are experts.

Isn't it funny that we pretend to know things inside out

When we barely even know them?

I know, your escape was the biggest mystery you
faced in your life,

But you always say that mysteries are what you are
thankful for.

What remains is a mirror, which may have been
shattered,

With pieces scattered throughout the box.

I want you to pick up the mirror and look deep
within yourself,

Try to dive into your eyes, into yourself,

Give yourself the freedom and time to know who is
in the reflection.

Your reflection is not just a reflection.

I know and trust that you will look at it really well.

Farther than the lines of your cheeks,

Farther than your shoulder bones because they are
so visible,

Farther than the curves of your body,

Farther than the polish of your nails,

Farther from your clothes.

Do not be afraid to dive into your depths,

To the point of exhausting your eyes,

To injuring your tongue, to healing your wounds,
to everything that does not exist.

These things require some appreciation and depth.

Superficiality is the killer of every riddle,

And the enemy of riddles is superficiality,

And you love riddles.

We both know you're not superficial.

Chapter 8 - Being Lonely and Being Alone

It was late at night, probably a Saturday, but he had stopped counting days long ago; it didn't matter anymore. There were no appointments worth remembering, no one worth meeting. He had just turned 28, but there was no celebration, at least not for him. He attended the gathering, but he wasn't really there. He wanted to end it, he hated every person in it… even those he usually liked. But most of the people who knew him did not care. All that was important to his so-called friends was that he would show up to work. To be fair, he wasn't quite emotional, and certainly, he did not like showing his emotions, but to miss his state of being, you had to be blind. Oh no, they all knew but did not care.

Every day was the same routine: he would go to work at the advertising agency, sign piles of papers that no one would read, and make a few calls to posh clients who rarely bothered to answer because they were busy with their own lives. Lunch was the only highlight of his day. After that he usually would go to check on a few of his men who were writing the papers he signed. Twice a week, sometimes even more he would go to a few of the agency's offices in different locations. He really wanted to go by car but his boss would only agree to pay for the train ticket, so that's what he did. In origin he was from some forgotten town in Canada but he had moved across the pond around a year or so ago. He'd never gotten used to the traffic moving in the other direction. He really hated that, and any big English city, and the food–he hated everything apart from reading (and his lunch).

One day he got a new destination to travel to, he was sent to Portsmouth. He really tried to be happy because it was the only city he liked in England. But no matter how hard he tried he just couldn't be happy.

It hadn't always been like this. It only started about a year and a half ago. Before that time he loved all his co-workers and he enjoyed his work even though it was dull. It was the same job but in canada. As a matter of fact he used to go out every few days. He was always surrounded by people all day long. He liked it, he lived like that for years, since school and college. He had one good friend, a girl around his age, and quite a few acquaintances. After all, he was quite a social and talkative person. His good friend was a tall and thin woman, around 25, who had met him in high school and since then they had been together. Even though they were quite different they had been to hell and back together. He liked going out as often as he could, while she enjoyed the comfort of her own fireplace and most impressive collection of novels. She preferred staying home because every occasion of the few times she actually went out somehow ended with the police involved. Once she drank too much and hit the barkeep. Another time she almost stabbed a waiter when running to the toilet. But the last time was when she got a bit drunk in an empty bar, (empty except for herself, the salesman, another colleague and another big man whom they did not know but who had introduced himself as John). That night she messed with some gangster, a friend of this John, who tried to steal a few bucks from the register. The robber did not see her 'bravery' in a kind way so he beat her until she lost consciousness.... Later when she gave her deposition at the police station she revealed that she had taken the gangster's watch and phone, which contained enough information to arrest about a dozen members of the gang. And so she was put under protective custody. But it all changed one day when she was killed, apparently by the gangster or someone in the gang who came to seek revenge.

At first, for a month, the poor salesman just sat at home doing absolutely nothing, but he was lucky enough to be understood: he wanted to be alone. And his friends let him, while constantly checking on him. That was until he decided to try and go back to society; though he had changed, it was alright. He started to value his privacy more and he started to take walks just to be alone at night, he tried to be happy, and for a few moments, though brief, he was. He had supportive friends and family, and he even enjoyed his alone time, it was then when he started reading partly in memory of his late friend, and partly as a way of escaping reality.

It was a few months after his friend's death, when he thought that he might just be okay, and life was as good as it could be under the circumstances. But he wasn't fine, nor was life. Every little thing drove him to a state of depression, he started crying, something he had never done before.

Finally he reached a point where he just couldn't stay in his small town in Canada. He just wanted out. He wanted out so badly that he asked for relocation, and so Headquarters moved him to Leeds, England. At first thought he thought that the move had helped but very quickly he learnt how wrong he was. It had all just gotten so much worse.

So there he was on a cheap second class seat, going to his favorite city, the one place where he could be happy. It was a long journey, so he was reading, until around six a big bulky man with blue eyes lightly touched his shoulder, saying 'excuse me?'

'Yes ?' he answered.

The man looked at him with his blue eyes and said 'don't you remember? From back in Canada?'

After a moment the salesman answered 'No, unfortunately I don't recall.'

'Oh, a pity, I am John Burnton.' The salesman replied 'Well when I think about it you do look familiar, but I can't remember where from, how are you anyway?'

Burnton turned around slightly and said 'I am alright, though I cannot say it about you from your look'

'Really? You can notice ?!' jumped the poor salesman,

'   Notice ?' laughed Burnton and said, a bit tactlessly, 'boy, everyone in that train can notice… it's about that dead friend of yours, right'

'Yes, it is about her'

'Well, here's what we will do, when this bloody train will stop I will show you around the city, to my flat and we will have a drink. Though I try not to… it got me in some troubles'

'   Thanks, I would like that. You know my friend always used to get herself in trouble when drinking, funny isn't it?'

'   Oh yes, coincidence' said Burnton 'well I have to go now, see you at the station'.

When Burnton left, the salesman remembered his old friend and the pain this caused him made him consider whether he should skip Mr. Burnton's opportunity. After all, he could not remember whether he actually knew him or not. But in the end he decided to try and meet him after all, and so he did.

After a few hours of walking through the streets of Portsmouth they were almost finished wandering, and for the first time in a long year and a half the salesman felt that he was not alone, he had grown to like this John Burnton. It was already past midnight when Burnton said 'here we go to the left and in 15 minutes we will be at my flat.'

They entered a dark small street between two car parks when John stopped, reached for his overcoat and said 'well I would like to apologize to you in advance.' His companion stopped, looking utterly confused.

'   Well, you see mate' John continued 'I never told you where we met. Do you remember that night at the bar with your friend?'

The salesman's heart sank as he finally remembered where he knew this John from. 'I'm the friend of the guy your buddy sent to prison for 15 years. And all that for some minor theft. We badly needed the money, you see, so we joined this stupid drug operation, and then your friend came and we became the reason the gang fell. He ended up in jail, somewhat safe, while I ran for my life from the rest of the gang. But here it ends: they caught me, it's me or you, they said. Either I shoot you, or they shoot me. I am truly sorry.'

As the salesman realized that he would not live for much longer he tried to beg, but that did not work. Finally, he said 'you know what is the funny thing here? Since she died, there was no one who understood me, no one to be there for me, until I met you on the train. I was so lonely yet surrounded by people at work, and now in this street? There is no one for me, yet I do not feel alone. I know I will meet her once more, do what you must, for God's sake.'

At that exact moment a gunshot was heard and the poor salesman fell down to earth. cold and bloody, but for the first time in what felt like a lifetime, somehow not alone. Entering a dark, narrow street between two parking lots, John suddenly stopped, reached inside his coat, and said, "I owe you an apology in advance."

Confused, the salesman stopped and asked, "What do you mean?"

"Well, you see," John began, "I never told you where we first met. Do you remember that night at the bar with your friend?"

A sinking feeling gripped the salesman as he finally remembered where he knew John from.

"I'm the friend of the man your buddy sent to prison for fifteen years," John explained. "It was over a minor theft. We needed the money, so we got involved with a drug operation. Then your friend intervened, and we became the downfall of the gang. He ended up in jail, somewhat safe, while I ran for my life from the rest of the gang. But it's over now. They caught up with me. It's either you or me, they said. Either I shoot you, or they shoot me. I'm truly sorry."

As the reality of his imminent demise sank in, the salesman tried to plead for his life, but it was futile. Finally, he said, "You know what's ironic? Since she died, there hasn't been anyone who understood me, no one to be there for me. Until I met you on this train. I've been so lonely, yet surrounded by people at work. And now, in this street, there's no one here for me, yet I don't feel alone. I know I'll see her again. Do what you must, for God's sake."

At that moment, a gunshot rang out, and the poor salesman collapsed, cold and bloody. But he somehow didn't feel alone for the first time in what felt like an eternity.

Chapter 9 - Poems from Gaza

The following poems were contributed by a talented young Palestinian writer in Gaza.

Sixteen became seventeen,

Living in Gaza, I'm keen

To be positive and just smile

But sometimes I can't for a while.

For now, a war has started anew

And the darkness in my spirit ensues.

But I will not let it break me,

Though it takes all of my energy.

My strength is like a rolling wave

That carries me through this stage.

I will not stop to smile and laugh,

And I will make sure to survive this path.

***

I feel a glimmer of something new,

A chance to start something anew.

A way to make a difference,

A path to create resilience.

Hope fills up my heart and soul,

It gives me strength to reach a goal.

To take a step, no matter how small,

To keep moving forward, one and all.

Hope gives me strength, hope gives me light,

To see the good in the darkest night.

To realize that all of us will survive,

As long as we keep hope alive.

Hope allows us to keep striving,

To never give up, even when we're tired.

To reach for the stars and never look back,

Hope, never let it lack.

***

He had been lost for so long, hidden away in the ground,

But he was found by a kind soul who saw something in his gaze,

And knew he deserved more than this dirty place.

The light in his eyes had never quite faded,

It was a beacon of hope that had been carefully shaded

From the darkness that had held him for so long

And could keep him safe in a world that felt so wrong.

He was scared and alone, his courage a fragile thing,

But the light in his eyes gave the stranger hope he'd cling

That the boy could find his way and discover his own strength

And make something of his life despite its length.

The stranger led him away to a better place,

Where he was loved, and nothing could replace

The kindness shown to him and the light in his eyes

That had shone like a beacon that day he was found.

Chapter 10 - Collaborative pieces

Pieces written by pairs of writers, often one Jewish and one Arab.

WE ARE FROM

In a world diverse, we find our birth,

From here and there, a place on Earth.

Women of the Mediterranean dream,

Hijabs and wigs, where self-esteem gleams.

A place that shines by candle's light,

Backgrounds varied in constant fight.

Beliefs and thoughts, day and night,

Arguments rise, yet share the same light.

To spread peace, canceling wrong by right,

To let coming generations think "no fight was here might."

A place where people yearn for peace,

Flying the love kite, wishing wars to cease,

Chasing butterflies and enjoying the swimming geese.

Daughters of Abraham, fighters bold,

Mothers, sisters, stories to be told.

Wives, lovers, and intellectuals too,

In a man's world, where hate they eschew.

Jews, Muslims, Israelis, and more,

Yet, women first, a truth to explore.

Defined not by nationality's decree,

A minority within minorities, we decree.

Equal rights, a question mark,

Women we are, leaving a lasting mark,

That will plant the light of hope and vanish the dark.

A 15-year-old, a mother, a teacher in one,

From different worlds, yet under the same sun.

Hand in hand, we try our best to realize a change was done,

And be proud to announce that, finally, evil was gone.

Swimming oceans, climbing each height,

Invisible warriors, challenging the night,

Till tiredness weakened the power and sight.

Voices unheard, long hair a threat,

Creators of life, we won't forget.

Doctors, historians, lawyers, we stand,

In the Middle East, a vast, diverse land,

To scream so high that we're together hand in hand.

Women of Peace and Equality's creed,

Dreaming of a day when war may recede.

In ears where our daughters may hold hands,

Non-judgmental souls, free in diverse lands.

Tamed by society, expectations' weight,

We question, doubt, and challenge the unseen fate,

Looking as far as we can to predict the next and balance the rate.

True believers in human rights so vast,

Jews, Muslims, Palestinians, women's rights amassed.

Feminism embraced, a blessing we hold,

Hips' curves, but brains' size, a story untold.

A stunning sight, the intellect's glow,

Women of substance, letting wisdom flow,

Teaching, searching, and talking to get the right through.

So much more, just wait and see,

Evil will be past, and haters will pay the fee.

Women of strength, we seem to be,

The hope for tomorrow and for treasure we are the key.

WE ARE FROM GIRLHOOD

You know how in the movies everything is perfect?

We are from girlhood.

We are from pink rooms and tutu skirts.

We are from pigtails and colorful nails.

We are from birthdays, HAPPY THEMED BIRTHDAYS.

We are from sparkly birthday tiaras.

We are from the candles' reflection in our eyes,

The candles that are waiting to be blown.

We stare at them with hope in our eyes, hoping that the next birthday will be better.

We are from trying to blow out candles and wishing,

Wishing change.

Change in our reflection.

But they're all different, right?

But what makes them different if in all of them, we want them to be different, we want something that we will never have?

We are from uncertainty; we don't even know what we want, changing our opinions every year, thinking we need to change, and hoping we'll change.

We are from trying to analyze ourselves.

We are from overanalyzing every move.

We are from fitting in, or maybe trying to.

We are from love and strength.

The strength of love, the strength of hate, the strength of judgment, the strength of empathy.

We are from the strength of love for everyone, but we forget someone along the road—we forget ourselves.

We are from shining eyes, wondering shining eyes.

We are from soft, shiny lips.

We are from untouchable but touched lips.

We are from dangerous bright red lipstick, but sometimes plain, boring lip oil.

We are from the desire—the desire of skinny, skinny arms, skinny legs, skinny habits, so skinny, stupid skinny, skinny as a strand of hair.

Our powerful weapon, the deadliest, the easiest to change, but the hardest—

Long, silky, flowy hair, blonde as gold, black as a midnight sky, brown as damp tree bark, red as our lipstick, our powerful red lipstick, and white as snow.

We are from vanilla and cookies whose smell makes the house dance,

From the smell of hot chocolate on a snowy day.

Warm, sweet, rich, and tranquil, making us confident that we are home, confident that others enjoy it as well.

Others enjoying how we smell; if we can't eat the cookie, at least smell like it.

We are from one cookie, one cookie that will make my silly, silky dress ugly.

We are from betrayal, a betrayal we chose, the battles we pick with that stupid silky dress.

We are from a box, pink Barbie box searching for our Ken.

Waiting to be picked, but we're not going to be because we're not a Barbie.

We are from the stereotypes of being pretty and stupid.

Or maybe stupidly pretty.

But smart and pretty is not the norm, not from the Barbie box, and we are the Barbie box.

When we finally reached the expected beauty standard of the world, we were knocked down by saying we're stupid because a girl can't be smart AND pretty.

We are death, breathing but not alive; we are all our problems. We suffocate ourselves, and when we're kind enough and alone, we let ourselves breathe, fearing being seen as extinct, as vulnerable.

We are from the sky; we're limitless, growing our wings as we grow and spreading them open when ready to realize we can fly. Realizing that no matter how much injustice there is in the world, that just means that we fight better than anyone because that's girlhood, that's being alive.

We are from the fear of life, or more specifically, birthing it. Not because of the pain (we're really strong, you know), but because of my daughter's

life, or the lack of it. We know our daughters would
have a difficult life; she would also like to be a
Barbie, you know? But you know how everything is
perfect only in movies?

However, we hope she'll change it and invent a
new Barbie—a Barbie that doesn't come in a box.

WE ARE FROM

In the dim, dreamy light, surrounded by the dark,

There stood two men in the middle of a park,

Discussing their nature as if it were a picture,

They both were talking one great mixture.

On a splendid journey, they are about to embark

From that dimly lighted place surrounded by the
dark.

"Where I came from, we can speak our mind,

Surrounded by friends in front and behind.

Where I come from, Jews can walk free,

Really, I give you my oath," said he.

"From two different places, I come, each one of a
kind,

Two places in me combined."

"I come from the land of the free,

Where you can be you, and I can be me.

A country founded on freedoms and liberties,

A city of immigrants and minorities.

I come from a place where Jews had the run of the
town,

A school that raised us up by putting others down,

A home where we were taught to respect and help
all,

A childhood of loving baseball and basketball.

I come from the world's biggest melting pot,

And 'went up' to share my people's lot.

How about you, my friend? Do state!

From where do you originate?"

"From two different kingdoms," the other one said,

Now, at war, for only one line of hate.

"How can I sleep? What will happen now?

I envy your peace; this I vow.

Yet when my eyes are closed,

The stars lead me to a different road.

To a third place, a different one, you see,

One that actually lets me be me, free.

The place where I grew up, the place where I fell,

This is home, I am sure, I can tell.

And though the arrows keep flying,

*If I were to say I'll go somewhere else, I would just
be lying."*

*And so the two men kept the talk for more than an
hour,*

Until they were left with no power.

And the sun came up, lighting the park,

Now, the two men no longer stand in the dark.

They left together and then said goodbyes,

Their paths are so different, yet intertwined.

*With dawn rising, they turned their backs on
yesterday,*

*And looked ahead to the future, for tomorrow was
now today.*

This We Are From poem was written in thanks to Professor Bob Vogel by the students who traveled to Philadelphia in April 2024:

WE ARE FROM

We are from the land of our forefathers

We are from pens and paper

We are from love

We are from passion

We are from our differences

We are from our similarities

We are from sadness

We are from laughing and crying laughing until we cry and crying until we laugh

We are from letter and words, beauty and pain

We are from overcoming fears

We are from insecurities

We are from creativity, imagination and fantasy, yet we live in a world that feels too real

We are from boundaries and restrictions

We are from tired of fighting

We are from fighting for our voices to be heard

We are from peace and fight, and from day and night

We are from silence

We are from chaos

We are from many traditions.

We are from many cultures

We are eight people

We are from seven languages.

We are from six cities

We are from five women

We are from four we are froms.

We are from three suitcases left in Spain.

We are from two religions

We are from one land

*We are from a land that was meant for peace but
has never seen the white dove.*

We are from here and there and everywhere

We are from the holy land.

We are from appreciation

We are from transformed lives.

*We are from expressing our deepest gratitude to
Bob.*

We are from Writing Matters.

Note: The following piece was written collaboratively with a Gazan friend. We wrote responsively – I wrote a line, then he wrote the next one, then I wrote, and then he did, alternating from beginning to end. We met online after October 7th through mutual friends.

I WONDER

I wonder

I wonder what life looks like from the other side

I wonder who I would be if I lived on the other side

I wonder if I'd be able to survive living in a society where you can't say what you think

I wonder if they think of me as a non-human

I wonder if there's anything I can say to make the situation better for you

I wonder if God tries to bring us closer together, but we can't see his signs

I wonder how people who are so good could end up with leaders who are so rotten

I wonder why people ignore our anger and despair

I wonder why it's hard for everyone to see the suffering on both sides

I wonder if my tears are less worth than theirs

I wonder what would happen if we treated each death as a human, without seeing sides

I wonder why Nakba is being denied

I wonder how we can escape the cycle of violence

I wonder how we can start trusting one another

104

I wonder what we can do to make our future better

I wonder if there's a future for my people

I wonder if our children will be able to wonder together in person

I wonder why you and me can speak this easily, without hesitation.

We wonder

Right Path, Wrong Time

Reader 1: The clock chased me, his hands running swiftly without stopping for a heartbeat.

Reader 2: With every passing minute, it got louder and closer.

Reader 1: TICK TOCK TICK TOCK

Reader 2: My good old friends' anxiety and stress, whispering in my ear, doing their job.

Reader 1: TICK TOCK TICK TOCK

Reader 2: Asking me for one thing, "be in control," but the pressure was getting to me as I waited to be free like a clock striking midnight.

Reader 1: STOP! Wait, that's not me! I don't break, I don't crack. I have all the answers and make all the decisions. It's a tiring job but it's always been me.

Reader 2: Me

Reader 1: Me

Reader 2: Me

Reader 1: Me, myself, and I, the number one priority.

Reader 2: Or at least that's how it seems.

Reader 1: How it seems to those who don't think like me, those who don't act like me, those who aren't me.

Reader 2: Those who stand aside and watch, the pawns not the players, the sheep not the shepherds.

Reader 1: But the shepherds stand alone, you see? Alone and confused, looking at the sheep, jealous of the uniformity.

Reader 2: So it's a curse you see to look down on people who aren't me. To believe my way is the only way.

Reader 1: It's a curse, you see, having the mind of the old but the body of the young.

Reader 2: It's a curse you see to be so stubborn at 15 when your thoughts are sprinting ahead while your body lags and everyone else seems to be moving at a different pace.

Reader 1: It's a curse you see being reminded that you're 15, that your ideas are equivalent to a baby's first step, exciting for the ones who have to be.

Reader 2: It's a curse, you see, a blessing disguised as a curse, one from whom I feed.

Reader 1: Feeding me, but it's never enough, leaving me crazy, craving more.

Reader 2: Knowing I need to stop, but I can't, and truthfully, I'm not so sure I want to. Reader 1: Because it's euphoric like ecstasy, a high as I stand, hallucinating superiority.

Reader 2: A validating drug that I can't help shooting in my brain.

Reader 1: And I can't help but question who the dealer was.

Reader 2: The one who sold it to me and not the other kids.

Reader 1: I watch as the clean kids walk with their high noses as I battle with sobriety.

Reader 2: Feeling sick as I detox.

Reader 1: As I detox THOSE feelings.

Reader 2: As I detox MY feelings.

Reader 1: The very ones who make me unique.

Reader 2: But that's just another word for the outcast.

Reader 1: Something I pray to God I won't be.

Reader 2: Asking "WHY ME?"

Reader 1: So it's an odd feeling, isn't it? Watching other kids who seem effortlessly carefree while we grapple with the weight of maturity.

Reader 2: Maturity that's my name, but I wish it wasn't because I needed to remember who I used to be.

Reader 1: I forgot what it means to be a kid, the simplicity and joy of not knowing.

Reader 2: And I can't help but feel out of sync amongst my peers.

Reader 1: Forgetting to breathe as I struggle to navigate simple conversions about stupid topics.

Reader 2: But they aren't stupid; they just sadly are no longer a fit for me.

Reader 1: TICK TOCK TICK TOCK

Reader 2: So, what is meant for me?

Reader 1: Am I on the right path? Living the life I desire? Or the life that was whispered in my ear and carved into the blueprint of my brain.

Reader 2: TICK TOCK TICK TOCK

Reader 1: They won't stop creeping in.

Reader 2: The questioning, the wondering, the doubts, and the regrets.

Reader 1: It's a cycle of overthinking and self-hatred.

Reader 2: A cycle I can't escape, no matter how much I scream.

Reader 1: But my screams go unheard because they aren't a cry for help.

Reader 2: They are a cry for peace of mind.

Reader 1: A cry for kids who grew up too fast and never sleep. Reader 2: TICK TOCK TICK TOCK

IT'S THEM

It's Sunday morning. I wake up, drool on my pillow, sheet marks scattered across my body, and my face still puffy. I turn on the TV to watch my favorite cartoon when I unintentionally see the news. I only linger for a moment.

On the news, they say it was them. How can I love them? They are the devil. How can I love them?

My friend Mohammad lost his parents in 2014; they were killed by a bomb. Before that, he used to be the life of the party, his smile shining bright and laughter filling my ears anytime I was around him. He loved soccer and playing "bananir" and "Omida."

He doesn't smile anymore, only the pitiful smile he gives to the people who say, "Sorry for your loss." He doesn't care about souls anymore; he doesn't believe everyone has them. I threw a ball at him and said, "Come on, let's play." He kicked it back like it was never a part of him and said to give it to a kid who would enjoy it. I think I saw a tear fall, but I didn't say anything because kids were orphaned all the time. Looking back now, I would have hugged him and told him everything would be okay. But that was a lie, and we both knew it even then… Ten years later, Mohammad was killed during the war. Then, I knew it would never be okay.

My friend Yoav lost his brother during the second intifada. He was always a quiet, kind kid and never let anyone fall behind. He loved to read books and go to the beach. He said he was at peace there. Yoav wanted to write books and travel the world.

Yoav is still quiet, but the kind of quiet that you notice, the kind that comes from people who have lost the will to say anything. He doesn't read books anymore because his brother would be the one to bring them to him. I don't remember the last time I saw him holding a book. Yoav doesn't come to the beach anymore. I wonder if he even has a place for peace. He doesn't travel. I think he felt guilty about traveling once his brother was six feet under. Looking back, I would have hugged him and told him everything would be okay. But that was a lie, and we both knew it even then... Twenty years later, Yoav was killed at the Nova party. Then, I knew it would never be okay.

Sometimes, I wonder how you expect us not to hate the very people who took everything away from us.

Even though he didn't get to be a therapist, Mohammad was my therapist. He never liked seeing me sad, so why leave? He taught me so much and even showed me how to love myself. He used to help his mom and everyone around him. When he was killed, I didn't just lose my friend or my therapist; I lost a part of me. A big part of me is with him in heaven. Maybe he can be that part's therapist.

Yoav was everything to me. He was like a brother. He wrote me little stories and held me up when life got tough. So why leave? Yoav was a pure-hearted boy. He wouldn't hurt a fly. And now he's up in the sky. My dear Yoav, are you looking down on me, guiding and protecting us?

Mohammad?

Yoav?

Just feel, take a deep breath, and let go.

Stretch your hand and lay your head on my chest over my heart.

Can you feel my heartbeat?

I can't feel yours.

Why can't I feel yours?

Can you hear me? Are you listening?

Are you there? Maybe if you don't have a rhyme, you can follow mine, the rhyme of love.

Love? I think I mean the rhyme of fear.

Eyes, beautiful eyes left open even when life went.

Ears clogged. Leave the ignorant bliss and educate yourself.

Stop hearing and start listening to me.

I will own up to my part in our story.

But stop hiding.

You are not innocent, a victim maybe, but you played a hand in your own downfall. Tongues, swear to God.

They spread empty promises and lie until those little white lies turn the tongue into black dust.

You promised a future, but Palestinians in Gaza fail to pass the age of 18. A nation of children who never grow up.

You promised a place where I could be me. Israeli Jews were massacred in their own country. A nation that has been slaughtered since the beginning of time.

Our senses make us senseless.

Paralyzed in fear like a child abandoned, angry like the breeze slapping the trees.

Two sides, always two sides, yet only one ever seen or one you choose to see.

Bleeding Hearts

A member of the people and cultural community whose traditional religion is Judaism and who traces their origins through the ancient Hebrew people of Israel to Abraham.

That is the definition of a Jew in the Oxford English dictionary.

I am a Jew.

In the sacred lineage of Shem, offspring of Abraham, twelve tribes, resilient and erect, proudly stand—survivors.

Four hundred years, the lash of whips upon our backs, our holiest temples shattered, dispersed in a diaspora, proselytizing in Spain, failed emancipation. The Russian Empire's dark massacre, Dreyfus falsely accused.

Your twisted accusations, a blood libel woven for our sacred rituals, a tapestry of make-believe. The awaited Messiah, a promise unfulfilled, Herzl's pen scribing truths, awakening our gaze, calling me a Zionist like it's an insult.

From 1933 to 1945, 6 million slaughtered, starved, and enslaved. Yet your ignorance and hatred roars, naming a genocide a holohoax.

Arab-Israeli, Six-Day War, Yom Kippur, and twice with Lebanon. The list goes on—a bittersweet story, stone-hard nationhood, a taboo word.

Men going to war like Ares, letting the women and children pay the price. You act like gods, but you're a man. Only a man. It's always a man who thinks he is a god.

I always get told, "You are the next generation," "Change the future." But how can I change the future when my very present is hell? How can I strive for greatness, goodness, lightness, and sweetness when all I know is pain?

113

Do we forgive and forget to achieve that "better future"? Or maybe just forgive in order to move past the pain? Because I will never forget; maybe we can be a voice for the people who seek healing, not revenge. A voice that understands reality yet has the people in mind and not brutality.

And fuck the people trying to gaslight me, claiming you're expressing a political opinion rather than bigotry.

"Clannish" is an ironic word when you force us to only associate with our own kind.

Claiming I'm a puppet master, but the puppets are going AWOL.

Cosmopolitan elite and Illuminati; I can't be discriminated against if I'm privileged.

Rothschild Soros never tasted respect—take their names out of your filthy mouth.

Calling for the globalization of the intifada, marking the homes of Jews, and ripping down posters. October 7, 2023, a date ingrained in my brain, blood, and bone. UN showing its true colors; the world is turning on its axis.

Mutilation and babies kidnapped, thousands dead, and we're still not one of the victims?

Sex used as a weapon, bodies cut like pieces of meat, young angels dancing to music traumatized.

Do you think the music was still playing in their heads as they hid for hours?

Judaism is an invitation screaming: Come abuse me!

Christians were deemed crazy, Muslims dangerous, but Jews were painted as Satan. September 11. Oh shit, it must have been a Jew.

Deadly Exchange. Oh shit, it must have been a Jew.

The deicide of Jesus. Oh shit, it must have been a Jew.

We are a scapegoat for the entire world.

The world is burning, and we are the fuel.

Yet, we are also the match, the ones who ignited it— No matter what step I take or how I take it, they seem to twist it.

Twisting truth left and right.

Calling me out on wrongs I have not committed.

When I am there, I am disturbing your society, and when I am here, I am ethnic cleansing, a place I also consider my birth land.

Yet, ironically, expressing dual loyalty is deemed a crime.

All I want is a place to call home. A place I could be me.

Wake up. Wake up, wake up. How did we get here? I don't understand. I'm just a kid. Why do they want my home, my country? We are such beautiful people.

But they could say the same. If only they could see, and I see them. See, my God promised me. I want answers, but all the adults seem to be asleep.

You could never understand me. I owe the brave souls who stood by me. But my pain is not mutual.

You can sympathize with me, but you cannot hold this generational burden.

It's a torch that was passed down that we all could not put out.

Just like the love, loyalty, and longing for Israel that will forever ignite.

I don't ask for your friendship, your acceptance, or your understanding.

I ask for basic human respect, from man to man, soul to soul.

I ask you to give us the right to live, to be free.

Empathy, basic human decency... where did it go?

Once a pillar, a foundation of human life has withered away. Society is corrupt, and human rights have become a privilege.

This is The Hunger Games, every man for themselves. And don't make alliances; they'll just betray you.

But is being alone better than working through the discomfort?"

Israel is a sanctuary for Jews in a world where you choose to hate.

Your actions have consequences, and you don't like the result.

You ask for my forgiveness, something very hard to give.

But forgetting is something no one will outlive. Unity and loyalty for our fallen brothers and sisters.

Pride, elegance, bravery, a fight for survival.

Pain, lessons, and the warmest community.

Strong spirits, unbreakable bonds,

An identity, an ancient tradition, morals, and ethics,

A chosen nation of God, a helping hand, and a loving nature.

That is the definition of a Jew to me.

Chapter 11 – Reflecting

A CHANCE TO WRITE ABOUT WRITING

While writing, I experimented and tried quite a few writing styles. I wanted to describe my thoughts and feelings on a given subject while not being confined to only one way of writing. I tried to write the piece that 'wrote itself' the best. I wanted to write in the style and way that felt the most suitable for each work while keeping track of which style, technique, and way of writing conveyed the best: both the general feeling I wanted the piece to have and the specifics of each work.

Overall, I like to think of writing as a way to store my thoughts, feelings, emotions, memories, and experiences in a more appealing way to an outsider. In other words, I see writing as a way to organize all that is going on inside my head in an easy-to-understand, approachable way for the future me, who might forget all the subtle context that may have been passing through these times.

At first, I came to this program with quite a few fears: 'How would I write if I haven't written any piece in my life?', 'How would I keep up with the group (I joined the course two weeks late)?', 'Is my English good enough?' and so many more questions. To be honest, I was almost scared to join the first Zoom call. However, in the first Zoom, it all turned out to be okay. Professor Vogel turned out to be one of the best teachers I have ever had. The English wasn't a problem (you get to write at your convenience, at your own speed, without anyone watching over your shoulder). And the fact that I hadn't written any piece beforehand turned out to be almost an advantage for me. After all, it is quite rare to get to draw on a completely clean canvas.

To be honest, I joined with a goal in front of me: I always wanted to write a book, and the few weeks before joining were spent seriously thinking about how to get started. When the opportunity came to join a writing course, I jumped on it, focusing on learning how to write a book. Little did I know, I have learned so much more than simply how to write. If anything, the most important thing that happened to me during the course was that I sat and just started writing for fun for the first time in my life. I experimented with a lot of styles, and although everything was a 'first time' for me, some things were 'first-er,' and I opened up to new styles.

Looking back just before the course, me thinking about starting to write and all the challenges that I would face, and looking at me now, writing this, I see one major difference. Suddenly, writing doesn't seem to be this scary, almost alienating thing that eventually creates a book. On the contrary, I have learned that writing is a process I enjoy and certainly will be doing more.

***

My name is Quds. I'm 17 years old, and I'm a Palestinian girl and an Arab. I was born and raised in Jerusalem. My parents named me Quds because of their love for Jerusalem. The first and quickest answer to the meaning of my name is the city, but it's so much more. In Arabic, "Quds" (قدس) also means something pure, holy, and beautiful.

I keep remembering how suitable it is for Jerusalem to have such a beautiful, pure, song-like name, how belonging and happy I feel walking in the old city, and how sad its beauty is. In my eyes, Jerusalem wins an award of the saddest beauty, the most exploited.

If Jerusalem were a person, it would have been a teenager, with the amount of conflict, self-battles, and trauma it holds. Jerusalem is the most experienced teen, even more than old "people."

With the right guidance, this teen can hopefully grow up into a stable adult. I hope that this lost, disturbed, beautiful, alluring teen can be guided. I hope that these conflicts never take over the teen but that the teen can get control over them.

My parents are originally from up north. My father is from a village called Nahef, and my mom is from Nazareth. I like writing a lot; it is one of my passions. It's very freeing; it is an art that speaks volumes. I'm now a senior in high school, and ever since elementary, I loved reading and writing. I found so much peace in them, in analyzing and getting into another's shoes and reading, understanding, or even trying to.

My writings each carry a piece of who I am, a different aspect. I keep saying that who I am is a broad question. A person is all that they are, all the groups, the labels, the stereotypes, the habits, the knowledge, the people they meet, the experiences they have, the love they share, how they love, how they feel loved, what inspires them, but I find the question taking another side. My situation is the only one that involves politics in the question, "Who am I?" Why is that? That is even more politics. I hope one day for a better reality.

I will finish with this: I heard a sentence once that goes, "Art should comfort the disturbed and disturb the comfortable," and if our pieces help disturb the comfortable (if the reality isn't already), I think we would have achieved something that might comfort the disturbed, and that might change something.

When we started the program, I was shy about sharing my most intimate thoughts, opinions, and words that I sometimes am afraid to tell myself. But I quickly learned that everyone with me in this course is doing the same, and I started to loosen up about it more.

The passion for the written word that everyone has is nothing short of contagious, and I believe it even pushes us to do better and achieve more. I had the pleasure of witnessing different kinds of writing and ways of expressing that others had/used that were really interesting. They even gave me ideas and encouraged me. The way everyone thinks differently is beautiful.

***

I grew up as a Jewish Italian-American New Yorker in Brooklyn, NY. On the morning of 9/11, I was an eighth-grade student. I remember how a regular school day soon became anything but ordinary—first, the rumors among students, rumors that were too crazy to believe, classes disrupted because of teachers who couldn't get to school, and finally, looking at the sky and seeing pillars of smoke rising from the direction of Manhattan.

On the morning of October 7th, I was an eighth-grade teacher. I remember how a holiday turned into a horror day—awoken abruptly by air raid sirens, rumors, and rockets flying as I went to synagogue, rumors that were too crazy to believe, celebrations dampened with so many men called up for another kind of service, and of course, looking at the sky and seeing not post-holiday fireworks, but smoke from the Iron Dome meeting Grad rockets in a fiery blast.

9/11 and October 7th happened decades and continents apart, but they have many parallels. Both are signposts in the memories of millions of people: Life before 9/11 and life afterward, life pre-October 7, and life post-October 7.

For me, the most meaningful thing that emerged from the ashes of 9/11 was the Jewish-Muslim basketball league that my dad and I helped organize to ease tensions in the ethnically and religiously diverse and divided Brooklyn of my youth. That small but brave step towards empathy and understanding set me on a path of building bridges with those from different backgrounds and bore fruit in the hundreds of students I have been able to bring together.

The most meaningful thing I participated in while still in the shadow of October 7th was the Writers Matter project that Professor Vogel and I helped organize to allow teachers and students in the ethnically and religiously intricate Israel of my adulthood to express their deepest emotions. That small but brave step of choosing to meet and open our hearts and minds to one

121

another via poetry and prose has already borne fruit in the powerful, stirring works that you have just read.

***

My name is Yara. I am a 16-year-old Palestinian girl living in Israel. I've always had a passion for writing because it's the only way that I can get things off my mind without feeling criticized. I never thought I'd share my writings with anyone, but joining this program gave me courage I didn't know I could have ever gained. As you can see, most of my writing talks about how much love I have for my nationality, and how nothing can take that love away.

What would you tell someone if they told you they want to join this program? I would look at them, smile, and remember all the beautiful things I wrote and the amazing things I've heard. I would tell them about the amazing opportunity that I, a Palestinian Arab, got, especially in a time like this when I couldn't find myself. I was scared to say anything that expressed how I felt because of the scary consequences I might have faced.

I would tell them how this program gave me the strength and courage to express myself freely and honestly. I wasn't scared because I knew I was surrounded by accepting and non-judgmental people.

I would tell them about how when I wrote with my Jewish partner, I felt the understanding and respect that we had for one another despite our differences and our pain for different people. It was still one pain that was killing us from the inside, and it was a pain that made us feel stronger together, a pain that gave us the need to change the situation we are in.

I would also mention the support that Steven, Robert, and my amazing peers gave me whenever I wrote something and read it out loud about the amazing feedback that Professor Robert was always ready to give without any hesitation. I would tell them how everyone should join a program like this because they won't be

122

scared or feel threatened by the other side, how in a program like this, they would grow in all kinds of ways, and how I guarantee they will love it as much as I did.

***

I am Maia Rachel Klara Assaf, a 15-year-old writer born in the vibrant heart of NYC. My roots are woven from Israeli, Moroccan, and Egyptian heritage through my father, while my mother brings the richness of German and Italian ancestry. I am a Jew. I am a girl. I am a writer. I've poured fragments of my soul into these words, expressing my deepest thoughts and emotions and sharing them with you. I hope my writing provides comfort, resonates with you, and makes you feel less alone. This is the inception of my journey as a writer, a path illuminated by honesty and the unsaid. A heartfelt thank you to the incredible group that brought this book to life—your support has not only made me a better writer but also a better person. With gratitude and love, Maia.

***

If you were to ask me whether diving into this writing course was a good idea, I'd say a resounding yes every single time without a moment's hesitation. Upon learning about the group, I initially harbored doubts about my writing capabilities. I questioned whether my knowledge and understanding were insufficient to partake in such an endeavor. However, I couldn't have been more mistaken.

What truly defines a writer? Is it someone endowed with an extraordinary imagination, a master of rhyme, or perhaps a skilled storyteller? To me, a writer is an individual armed with a pen, paper, and a voice eagerly awaiting its moment of expression. A writer isn't confined to a singular ideal image; rather, it is someone with a message to convey. And that's precisely who we are—a collective of diverse yet kindred spirits, individuals who were once silenced but discovered the profound beauty within the strokes of a pen.

123

This group serves as a sanctuary devoid of judgment and brimming with unwavering support. We are united by a shared appreciation for the unique beauty embedded in each other's creations. In our midst, there is no room for harboring resentment or anger. Instead, we've come together with metaphorical white flags adorning our backs, ready to write—to compose our own peace treaty. And therein lies the beauty of it all—those seemingly inconsequential words, inked by teenage girls, have metamorphosed our entire relational landscape.

When articulating your emotions becomes a formidable task, writing becomes the conduit that extracts those words from the depths of your being. This group, therefore, is not merely an assembly; it is a gift—a treasure that I shall forever hold in reverence, elevated on a pedestal that symbolizes my ongoing journey of self-discovery and enlightenment. This transformative experience is one from which you can only stand to gain. I implore you: whenever the fear of failure looms large, that is precisely the moment to take that crucial first step.

This group embodies an amalgamation of emotions—it's daunting, exhilarating, enchanting, and eye-opening. Yet, above all, it is extraordinary. Surrender to the guidance of the pen, and you'll find your mind effortlessly following suit.

Chapter 12 - Our Students

Steven used two prompts, "I Am From" and "I Wonder," with 4th-10th grade Druze, Muslim, and Christian students from the Maghar English Leadership program and Jewish and Eritrean students from Krol Elementary School and The Chen Young Ambassadors School.

I AM FROM

I come from a family that loves sports.

I come from an old country.

I come from a good school.

I come from a family that believes in Jesus.

I come from a Jewish country.

I am from Eritrea.

I come from a rich country.

I come from a family that loves me.

I come from a family where mom and dad are important.

I come from a good and kind family.

***

I am from Israel.

I am from liking to play with my family and friends.

I am from learning in a good school.

I am from liking to study about the United Nations.

I am from a big city in a small country.

I am from liking to read books.

I am from liking to watch the news.

I am from being interested in history.

I am from making good videos for my YouTube channel.

I am from liking to eat steak.

***

I come from a bad place.

I come from a place that loves music.

I come from living with three people: my mom, my sister, and my uncle.

I come from my mom and dad getting divorced when I was three years old in Tel Aviv, and three years later my sister was born.

***

I come from Holon.

I come from a place where I have many friends.

I come from a lovely family.

I come from a Jewish country.

***

I live in Israel.

I have one sister.

I have two hamsters.

***

I come from living in Israel, but I'm Eritrean.

My parents come from Eritrea.

I have a sister, but she is not living with me; she is in Uganda. I have never seen her, but that is not important.

***

I come from Israel.

I was born in a hospital.

I come from having a lot of friends.

126

I come from a nice school.

I come from working hard for my dreams.

***

I come from being the only boy in the house.

I come from being in a family that shows love.

I come from a family that helps.

I come from a house with not much.

I come from a house with great food.

I come from a house of honesty.

I come from being weak to being strong.

I come from being the only child to being with four kids in the family.

***

I come from one sister and one brother.

I come from a sports family.

I come from a safe city.

I come from Eritrea.

***

I come from Ukraine. I live in a Ukrainian family.

I come from dancing ballroom dance—I'm a double Israel champion for ballroom dance.

I come from a place that has war.

I come from a cold place.

I come from a place with a beautiful language.

I come from loving my life.

***

I am from living in Israel.

I am from loving to study Math and English.

I am from loving computer games.

I am from loving my family.

I am from a big house with a kitchen and four bedrooms.

I am from having two sisters and two brothers and a big family.

I am from loving to eat special chips.

***

I am from living in Israel.

I am from loving to study Math and English.

I am from loving computer games.

I am from loving my family.

I am from a big house with a kitchen and four bedrooms.

I am from having two sisters and two brothers and a big family.

I am from loving to eat special chips.

***

I lost a dog when I was four.

My nickname is Igomgam.

I love animals.

My favorite place to go is Paris.

I am nine years old and in the 4th grade.

I'm in a family of nine members.

I want to have another pet. And I want a cat.

I want to be the perfect one in the family so that my mom will love me the most.

I like stories.

I have a lot of makeup.

I like English classes.

My height is 150 centimeters (or something like that).

Sometimes my big brother annoys me (a lot!).

Some of my classmates think that I am not from Israel, but it is not true.

I remember from my childhood how my dog died and I am still sad about it.

In kindergarten, there was a bully and she bullied me every day, so I am happy that she is not in my new school.

Dogs are my favorite animal.

I want to be a vet.

***

I am from being nine years old.

I am from loving animals (almost all kinds).

I am from not liking bugs.

I am from not liking stupid commercials.

I am from not liking loud and noisy places.

I am from loving traveling.

I am from having two cats.

I am from not liking trashed places.

I am from loving books.

I am from loving baking.

I am from hating my mom shouting.

I am from liking comedies.

I am from loving flowers.

I am from learning languages.

I am from wondering what I will look like when I'm eighteen.

I'm from being future-phobic.

I am from loving fruits (especially mangoes).

I am from liking fairy tales.

I am from liking theaters.

I am from loving circuses.

I am from wanting to work in a zoo.

***

I come from two sisters in the house.

I come from a good and safe place.

I come from a big family.

I come from a better school.

I come from being an older boy.

I come from Eritrea.

***

I AM FROM

I come from my granny dying when I was eight years old and she was sixty-four years old.

I come from my dad not liking a lot of hair and my mom adoring long hair.

I come from my favorite subject in school being English, loving sports, and my favorite animal being a cat.

I come from my sister adoring me so much.

I come from wearing matching colors with my sister.

I come from a mom who loves to spoil me, but she only buys me what.

I WONDER

I wonder if everybody woke up happy and never was sad.
I wonder what if humans couldn't make mistakes.
I wonder what will happen ten years into the future.
I wonder, if no one could hide their feelings, where would society be now.
I wonder, if the coronavirus never happened, would everyone be happier or sadder.
I wonder what if the poles are not melting and climate change never happened.
I wonder how the world would be now if everyone listened to everyone.

***

I wonder how aquatic beings breathe.

I wonder if animals understand humans.

I wonder if my little sister understands what I'm saying to her.

I wonder how Mercury, which is closer to the sun, is not the hottest planet.

***

I wonder why can't all the people in the world be good.
I wonder why there are still wars.

***

I wonder what my job would be.

I wonder where I will live in the future.

I wonder what I will eat for breakfast.

I wonder if I will ever fly on a plane.

I wonder how it feels to be a younger sister.

I wonder why my mom will have a car.

I wonder if I'm gonna be rich.

I wonder if I'm gonna be a pro dancer.

I wonder if I will have a dog.

I wonder if I'm gonna be popular.

***

I wonder if I will win a Fortnite tournament.

I wonder why the leader of North Korea doesn't let people go to other countries.

I wonder why Hitler hated Jews.

I wonder where I am gonna work.

I wonder if God is real.

I wonder how it feels to be rich.

***

I wonder if Ronaldo will win the World Cup.

I wonder how much time is left for me.

I wonder if I will be a professional footballer.

I wonder if there are dinosaurs.

I wonder if I will have a wife.

I wonder how many kids I will have.

I wonder if I will be a good father.

I wonder how many Christians there are in the world.

I wonder if God will help me.

***

I wonder what will happen if we could go back in time.
I wonder what if everybody could fix their mistakes.
I wonder how people would feel if they were not mistaking life.
I wonder if it is possible to do that.
I wonder if there is someone controlling us.

132

I wonder what aliens would think about us if they met us.

I wonder how we would feel about not being able to feel pain and becoming immortal.

I wonder what we would do if we got this power.

And I wonder if that's gonna end the existence of the world.

***

I wonder if tomorrow the war ends, if an alternative to it will be peace.

I wonder what life would be like if there were six months of rain and storms and six months of sun.

I wonder how pupils would be if they always studied through distance learning education without returning to school.

***

I wonder what is your favorite sport.
I wonder what is your favorite season.
I wonder what makes you happy.

***

I wonder what I'm going to eat today.

(I think it's eggs)

I wonder what my friends are doing right now.

(I think they are learning)

I wonder what it feels like to be alone.

(It probably feels sad because you don't have friends)

I wonder what it feels like to have a sister.

(It probably feels boring)

I wonder what it feels like to be a teacher.

(I think it feels like something fun)

I wonder what it feels like to die.

(It feels like crying sad)

133

I wonder what it feels like to be rich.

(It feels fun because I can buy my family a present)

I wonder what my family is doing.

(My mom and dad are working; my brother is playing)

I wonder what my brother is doing in daycare.

(I think my brother is playing at the daycare)

I wonder what my dad is going to give me as a present for my birthday.

(I hope a PS5)

***

I wonder what do you want to be in the future.
I wonder what is your dream for the future.
I wonder why did you choose this profession.

***

I wonder if the world is going to end.

I wonder if people could fly.

I wonder if dogs had superpowers.

I wonder if boys had long hands.

I wonder if fish could breathe on land.

***

I wonder who will win the World Cup.

I wonder if there will be World War 3.

I wonder how many people there are in the world.

I wonder how many people will die.

I wonder how much time I have in life.

I wonder if I will be a football player.

I wonder if I will be a millionaire.

I wonder if I will have a wife.

I wonder if I will have kids.

I wonder if I will be a good father.

I wonder if we have dinosaurs in the world.

***

I wonder how an eagle can build its nest on top of the mountains at a height that reaches the clouds and simultaneously see creatures that crawl on the ground.

***

I wonder how to become an English teacher.

***

I wonder what cars will look like in the future.

I wonder if people will live on the moon and other planets.

I wonder if people will evolve to adapt to other kinds of air.

I wonder what would happen if we all lived in harmony.

I wonder what's on the other side of a black hole.

***

I wonder if I'm gonna succeed.
I wonder why people sweat.
I wonder how school was invented.
I wonder how the past was, back when they had dinosaurs.
I wonder how school was in the past.
I wonder how sports were invented.
I wonder how people get bored.
I wonder if there are clowns (the scary kind) in Israel.
I wonder how people become popular.
I wonder how people can laugh at jokes that aren't funny.

***

I wonder (to future me) why you chose this job.

135

I wonder where are you going to study for this job.

I wonder how long it takes to study this subject.

***

I wonder if there are aliens on Mars.
I wonder if there are people who like to eat monkeys.
I wonder if there were no wars, just peace in the world.
I wonder if I wake up tomorrow and I find that people help each other.
I wonder if the world will be better in the future.
I wonder if Argentina will win the World Cup in 2026.

***

I wonder if my father goes to the IDF, what will I feel?

I wonder if there were no wars.

I wonder what would happen if we stopped drinking water.

I wonder how a plane flies.

I wonder how oil gets out of the olives.

***

I wonder what your favorite fruit is.

I wonder what I want to be in the future.

I wonder what your favorite PlayStation game is.

***

I wonder if there were no limits between countries and people could travel wherever and whenever they wanted!

***

I wonder how the kidnapped women arrived in Gaza, what fear and pain they were feeling, and how the destructive terrorists were dealing with them. Did they torture them or feed them, and did they take care of the children or torture them?

I hope that the war will end, we will return to our normal lives, and all the kidnapped people will return to their homes safely.

***

I wonder if all the people are good or bad.

I wonder if after many years we will still have wars.

I wonder if we don't kill animals if there would be a lot of animals.

I wonder if after 100 years we will have peace.

I wonder if we can be heroes after many years.

***

I wonder why did you choose this job.

I wonder where did you learn that?

I wonder did any of the family learn this work?

***

I wonder why did you choose this God.

I wonder if your dream is to be a doctor?

I wonder which kind of doctor you want to be.

***

I wonder what do you want to be in the future.

I wonder what you like to play?

I wonder if you speak English well?

***

I wonder what do you want to become and why.

I wonder what is your favorite drink.

I wonder what is your favorite color.

I wonder where you would like to travel.

137

I wonder what is your favorite animal.

***

I wonder which sports you like.
I wonder which games do you like.
I wonder what are your dreams when you get
older.

***

I wonder how you imagine technology in 2050.

I wonder what you want to be when you grow up.

I wonder if you will travel next summer?

***

I wonder what you do in your free time?
(I play football)

I wonder what is your favorite animal.
(Mine is a horse)

I wonder what is the name of your school.
(Mine is Elementary school)

***

I wonder why the President of Eritrea doesn't let
people leave the country.

I wonder what I could see if I put my eye in the Red
Sea.

I wonder where the snow comes from.

I wonder why I don't have a passport.

I wonder why Hitler hated the Jewish people.

I wonder how it will feel to be famous.

I wonder how it will feel to have presents.

I wonder if I will see God one day.

I wonder how to be a manager of engineering.

I wonder why college exists.

Chapter 13 - Peace

Students (ages 9-17) from four religions in Israel and Gaza were asked to define peace.

Students in Gaza

1. Peace, to me, means that I can move freely where I want. I will not be afraid anymore. Not losing my mom and dad and sister and brother because of an airplane attack. And not be hated because I am Palestinian.

2. When I do not need to be afraid because of the bombing and shooting, and I can live wherever I want.

3. Peace to me means to not be afraid anymore that I have to go to bed and wake up from bombs. Or be afraid of losing those who matter to me.

4. To me, it means to be without trauma, nightmares, triggers, PTSD, and no more fear. And that there is trust enough to meet.

5. To get away from the vicious circle of war, and revenge, and just be free and be whoever and wherever I want. Absence of fear.

6. To me it means when wars are over and we can trust one another. And [we can shed] tears from other things, not from war. When the circle of violence is destroyed.

7. Peace to me is when seeing an airplane doesn't instantly make me scared. But rather wonder where the people in it are traveling. Something I have never seen. It is also to feel safe enough to sleep without wondering if I will ever wake up again or if I will die in the rubble of my own home.

8. Peace to me is when I can rest in Islam's arms and truly appreciate Allah's creation's beauty. Peace to me is when the

child is loved and safe no matter where a child is born. And the child won't be an orphan because of war. Peace to me is when we all can accept one another as human beings. Then, we can truly find inner and outer peace.

9. Living in peace means to exist without fear of anything – fear of losing loved ones, fear of not achieving goals, fear of having one's rights and dignity violated. Peace is learning to love others despite their differences and wishing them well. Love is peace.

Jewish Students in Israel

D: An agreement between two countries not to fight. When there's hardship, to help one another. To visit one another.

E: The absence of war or conflict among major international powers.

A: It's like when 2 kids are fighting and they decide to make peace among them, it means that they won't fight from now on.

E: Peace means no war, no crying, no anger. It means an agreement between two sides and cooperating towards a common goal.

N: Unity

A: The feeling that I can live without fear that something bad will happen. That I can move around the country or the world without the fear that they will try to do something to me because I am Israeli or Jewish. Life without another round of bombs every few years. That we won't have to run to shelters or hear on the news on a daily basis that there was another attack, or that people were murdered in the street. Just think of security.

T: Diplomatic relations; the opposite of war.

N: Opposite of a state of war.

S: Love for everyone, to be there for the other, and to respect everyone, how they are, regardless of background.

Y: An agreement between countries to stop fighting, and the countries eventually become friends.

I: An agreement between countries.

N: Shalom/Peace is a greeting between people or an agreement between countries.

B: Peace to me is really when people get along with each other

O: When two countries are not fighting and instead work together in partnership

N: When two countries are fighting and they reach a peace agreement so that people in their countries can live in security. Peace is a word that connects people. God willing it is possible to find solutions.

E: Peace means going to the bomb shelter less. More life, less violence, more understanding, and love between people. It's better for everyone and fun for everyone.

M: To live in partnership with everyone.

C: Wow, that's a really hard question to answer. For me, it is just to know that everyone is doing great and more of it actually feels good. That is, anyone is believing and doing what they want. For example, one of my goals is to seek inner peace (to be happy with things that I achieve).

Y: An agreement between two countries to be in peace and not attack one another. To divide the land and not fight over it.

B: No wars; quiet.

S: A situation where two sides don't fight and there is no hate between people.

I: Everyone loves one another, and there's no fighting over anything.

Y: Countries that don't fight one another.

T: A state of non-conflict that happens when two world leaders meet in the same place and then talk until they reach an agreement.

O: When you respect one another, each with different practices, religions, cultures, customs, and views, and when you also help one another.

N: Peace is like reconciliation between friends. Or a conflict between countries that is resolved through negotiation, for example, the situation we are in now of war, because, of course we will eventually reach peace.

Y: In Israel, a country surrounded by enemies, peace is not something to be taken for granted. We've found ourselves at war against one or more countries numerous times, and now we are in a war against the terror organization Hamas. War seriously impacts how the country functions since so many resources are diverted to fighting the war. For example, the Israeli economy is hurt because so much must be spent on military equipment. Moreover, war causes many civilian and military casualties. In conclusion, peace between countries is very important, and we need to make peace in order to know that we are protected.

Christian, Druze, and Muslim Students in Israel

B: Peace is freedom.

A: When there is no war, and all the countries will compete in sports competitions together.

S: Instead of violence between people, there is stability and security.

A: Everything good.

143

S: Living in peace, with safety, love, respect, and life without war.

M: I dream about a world without war. I hope there is no hate between people. I hope that everyone wishes the best to one another, helps, and loves one another.

A: Peace is a healthy relationship between people and two countries.

L: Peace is a beautiful, secure life without fear and anxiety about the future. Peace means love, closeness, and a happy life free of wars and children's fears.

T: Peace means different things to different people and cultures. But in my own words, Peace means living our lives selflessly and treating others with respect.

M: Peace is a word that indicates love and safety between people. No fear or violence, but respect and protection for people.

A: Love and accepting the other.

R: Peace for me is humanity first because if humanity is present, hatred disappears, and people live together with love. I hope that peace prevails for everyone and that wars disappear.

A: Peace is when all the countries are tolerant of each other and there is no war.

N: For me, peace means no war in the world and peace among people.

M: Peace be upon me. Peace is to live in security in general, freedom among all the people in the world, and freedom to express opinion. Peace is inner peace. For a man to be reconciled with his fellow man.

R: Peace is when all the countries stop fighting.

H: People are happy, and people feel safe; they are not scared. Pupils go to school; parents go to work. We are free, and people can go anywhere they want.

S: Peace is a situation of calm and safety for all the people around the world.

A: When I think of peace, I think of the dove and the branches of the olive tree. I imagine a beautiful world, but politics runs the world so far, and peace depends on the world's leaders. But we can change that. We, the kids of today, will be the adults of the future, so we have a responsibility to bring peace and prevent wars.

T: Stability, safety, reassurance, love between countries.

N: Peace, for me, means that there is Peace between all countries, there are no wars, all people love each other, and there is no violence among them.

N: Forgiving and Accepting others.

R: No wars. The people are good.

J: What do I think about peace? That is an unusual question. As I think more about it, peace is something that is difficult to receive. If war ends and we are free to go wherever we want. Why can't this happen? This could be real if people are not aggressive and evil anymore. We can't control minds, but if teachers at school or parents at home around the world taught kindness and love and that we would be one team to save the planet and the world, then peace could come true, like in a dream.

O: Everyone living with no crimes or war or anything like that.

M: Peace is security and goodness for humans and the world.

K: Peace is a state of stability and reassurance that society and individuals experience and the individual enjoy. He enjoys all his rights, duties, and obligations without pressure or coercion.

R: Quietness.

A: No wars.

R: No wars. No violence, and People love each other.

L: Peace means people love, accept, and respect each other. Countries are in good relationships.

Chapter 14 - Looking to the Future

OUR PLANS FOR EXPANDING THE WRITERS MATTER PROGRAM

As the organizers of this project, we didn't realize how meaningful it would become. When we started, most participants kept their cameras off during the Zoom sessions and hesitated to share. Within a few weeks, everyone wanted to share their writing and hear one another's pieces. As the time flew by, our weekly hour-long session often extended well into a second hour.

Each week, we were amazed anew at the emotions and ideas that appeared in participants' writing—the raw pain, fear, hopes, compassion, and empathy as the writers attempted to make sense out of insanity, to find humanity in this maze of man-made chaos.

Sometimes it's easier to express difficult, personal and sensitive ideas in writing. That's what was so helpful in using the Writers Matter process—sitting down and writing things that everyone had inside, getting things off the chest through writing. Those ideas and emotions are as important for each of us to express as they are for others to hear.

This context also helped us listen, hear, and feel. Observing the echo chambers and polarization on social media and what public discourse has descended into all around the world, it seems like many people, even those who are thousands of miles away from the conflict, can't feel empathy for both Israeli Jews and Palestinians at the same time. There is just not much space to acknowledge that people on the other side are suffering as well. But when we wrote and shared together, it quickly became obvious that as with so many other issues, we have this in common. All of us, both people living in the Holy Land, are victims of this conflict. That empathy is a strength of the program.

Maybe the best part was the "We Are From" exercise. It seemed daunting—writing with someone who you've only met recently, from a vastly different background, about what you have in common. But once again, every group gave it its own personal touch, and the end results were just amazing, proof that together, we are even greater than the sum of our parts.

The powerful pieces written during the project and the deep meanings and emotions they contain have touched hundreds of people already. Our trip to the US reached over 500 people of all ages, and the writing shared on our blog has reached over 1,000 viewers. We have already begun expanding the project—working with teachers from a dozen communities within Israel on a two-month teacher training project, culminating in a two-day writing retreat. We are also planning a peer-led writing workshop for Druze, Christian, Muslim, and Jewish students to extend this program to reach hundreds more students. In the coming weeks, we will launch an annual writing competition, the first of its kind, open to Jewish-Arab writing teams, with prizes for the winners.

We hope you have been as moved by these pieces as we have and that it inspires you to start your own writing journey. Empowering students and allowing their inner voices to be heard can make all the difference for a better tomorrow. Please reach out and mention a specific piece that touched you or suggest ideas for future projects. You can reach us at:

vogel@lasalle.edu | Debateforpeacemun@gmail.com